Anselm: A Very Short Introduction

VERY SHORT INTRODUCTIONS are for anyone wanting a stimulating and accessible way into a new subject. They are written by experts, and have been translated into more than 45 different languages.

The series began in 1995, and now covers a wide variety of topics in every discipline. The VSI library currently contains over 700 volumes—a Very Short Introduction to everything from Psychology and Philosophy of Science to American History and Relativity—and continues to grow in every subject area.

Very Short Introductions available now:

Available soon:

For more information visit our website

www.oup.com/vsi/

Thomas Williams

ANSELM

A Very Short Introduction

Great Clarendon Street, Oxford, OX2 6DP,
United Kingdom

Oxford University Press is a department of the University of Oxford.
It furthers the University's objective of excellence in research, scholarship,
and education by publishing worldwide. Oxford is a registered trade mark of
Oxford University Press in the UK and in certain other countries

First edition published in 2022

Impression: 1

Published in the United States of America by Oxford University Press
198 Madison Avenue, New York, NY 10016, United States of America

British Library Cataloguing in Publication Data

Data available

Library of Congress Control Number: 2022938890

ISBN 978-0-19-289781-7

Printed in the UK by
Ashford Colour Press Ltd, Gosport, Hampshire

Contents

List of illustrations

Chapter 1
Anselm's life, work, and contexts

In September of 1092, a 59-year-old Benedictine abbot, well-known for his theological acumen and his spiritual guidance to kings, nobles, priests, and monks, found himself in England, attending to the overseas dependencies of his abbey in Normandy. It was a somewhat tricky time for Abbot Anselm to be in England, because he was in the eyes of many the obvious successor to his former teacher Lanfranc as archbishop of Canterbury, and Anselm did not want to appear to be angling for the job. Nonetheless, his business in England was pressing, and so he went.

Lanfranc had died more than three years earlier in May of 1089, but the king, William II, had not appointed anyone to succeed him: it suited the king to keep bishoprics vacant so that he could use church revenues to fund his military operations in Scotland and Wales. He felt no urgency about naming a new archbishop until March 1093, when he fell ill; fully expecting to die, he wanted to get right with God and the church while he had time. The royal court was then at Gloucester, and, as it happened, Anselm's business in England had taken him to a village nearby. So Anselm was summoned to administer last rites and hear the king's confession. It may be that a promise from the king to fill the vacant archbishopric was a condition of absolution—we can't really know that part—but certainly the topic arose, and the king immediately named Anselm as his choice.

1. Anselm resists being named archbishop of Canterbury by an ailing William II.

Anselm was horrified. He begged, pleaded, wept, protested—his biographer tells us that Anselm's nose bled from the stress—but to no avail. The king and bishops, even Anselm's own retinue, insisted that he accept. Anselm clenched his hand to avoid receiving the pastoral staff that the king was trying to thrust upon him, so the bishops pried his fingers apart and then closed them around the staff (see Figure 1). Anselm was carried into the church to shouts of acclamation and the singing of hymns, while he kept protesting *Nihil est quod facitis*: 'This is nothing, what you are doing'. But however desperately Anselm may have wished that it all come to nothing, he was not to have his way, and by August of 1093 he had accepted the archbishopric of Canterbury. It would prove to be a vexatious job in many ways, but he held it for the rest of his life.

Besides being one of the crucial turning points of his life, Anselm's accession to the archbishopric of Canterbury illustrates the multiple contexts in which his life and his work must be understood. He was a monk, committed to the Rule of Saint Benedict and the rigorous demands it made; he wrote and taught within that monastic context, not as a freelance teacher who gathered students around himself (there were many such teachers in those days), but also not in one of the cathedral schools that would eventually develop into universities. He was a public figure who corresponded with monks and laypeople alike, addressing matters of controversy, dispensing spiritual counsel (sometimes unasked-for). As archbishop he was drawn into the turmoil of church–state relations and was an important figure in the church's attempt to wrest control away from kings and nobles. Thanks to Lanfranc's teaching he was initiated into the intellectual mainstream of his day, though he carried out his philosophical work in such an individual way that he broke intellectually—though never personally—with Lanfranc. I will examine these contexts—monastic, intellectual, public, and ecclesiastical—with a view to showing how understanding them sheds light on Anselm's life and on his writings.

The monastic and intellectual contexts

Not even the most admiring of hagiographers—and we have such a person in the figure of Anselm's friend, disciple, and biographer Eadmer—would pretend that Anselm had always been drawn to the monastic life. An intense desire at the age of 14 to enter a monastery, thwarted by the local abbot, soon faded. Anselm turned to ordinary pursuits, not particularly devout but also not particularly dissolute, lest he displease his pious and doting mother, Ermengarda. When she died, around 1050, Anselm was bereft. Anselm's father, Gundulf, never the easiest of men to get along with, became unbearable; in 1056 they quarrelled irreconcilably, and Anselm left the family home in Aosta to make a new life elsewhere.

What exactly he was looking for, or indeed whether he was looking for anything in particular at all, is unclear. We know that he travelled through Burgundy, the Loire valley, and Normandy, where there were both schools and monasteries of great renown; but we do not know whether he sought any of them out. After three aimless years he at last found a direction: he went to Bec to study with the great Lanfranc.

Lanfranc was prior of the abbey and the head of its school, which at that time was open to external pupils, sons of the nobility and gentry who were to be educated in the liberal arts for careers in a world that increasingly rewarded facility with the written word, as well as clerics eager to learn from someone who 'relit the light of the arts in the West', 'whom God raised up to be a guide and a light to lead the minds of the Latins'. External pupils brought in money, and the abbey was prosperous. Lanfranc managed much of its external business and had become a trusted adviser to William, duke of Normandy.

Lanfranc's scholarly reputation was founded in particular on his mastery of dialectic, the use of techniques of linguistic analysis and logical argumentation to clarify philosophical problems and to elucidate answers. The great historian William of Malmesbury wrote that Lanfranc 'sent out his pupils into the world belching forth dialectic'. There was something of a mini-renaissance of dialectic in the 11th century, although it's not entirely clear why. Generally when a new burst of philosophical energy emerges, it has some discernible cause: new texts become available, new logical techniques are developed, scientific developments push people to think in new ways. But in the 11th century people had all the same old texts, used all the same old logical techniques, made no new scientific discoveries of note. Yet for some (or no) reason there was a revival of dialectic, and Anselm came on the scene as the revival was in full flower. No doubt it was not the monastic life that drew him to Bec, but the opportunity to learn from the greatest of the dialecticians, Lanfranc of Bec, who might well

4

be known as the preeminent figure of the 11th-century intellectual scene if Anselm hadn't entirely eclipsed him.

Anselm arrived at Bec in 1059. He fell into a sort of hero-worship of Lanfranc, who in turn recognized Anselm's ability and soon gave him a share in the teaching. Anselm took quickly and naturally to the intellectual life that Lanfranc had created at Bec. The monastic life was more of a struggle, but after some hesitation (and, one is tempted to say, a bit of self-created drama) Anselm did take his monastic vows in 1060. However tumultuous the path to commitment had been, the commitment itself was wholehearted and irrevocable.

Monastic life shaped Anselm's thought in certain obvious ways: he developed arguments in conversations with fellow monks; he wrote some works at their request or for their use; his correspondence is filled with pastoral advice to monks and nuns about how to live out their monastic profession. More striking, however, are the ways in which his monastic embrace of obedience, authority, and common life arguably shapes even his treatises. For Anselm there is freedom in obedience and the acceptance of authority: no longer a slave to his own desires, no longer burdened with the need to make his own way in the world, a monk attains the liberty to focus wholeheartedly on God. And this is true not only in the domain of action but also, perhaps preeminently, in the domain of thought. Acceptance of theological authority is not a straitjacket; it does not inhibit creative thought, but sets one free to think about 'the deep things of God' with confidence that one's thinking will not go off the rails.

There is even a tantalizing suggestion in Anselm's letter *On the Incarnation of the Word* that obedience, spiritual discipline, and meditation on Scripture—the core of the monastic life—can enable someone to *experience* the truths of faith. 'Experience' (*experior*) is a word Anselm uses for first-hand acquaintance with something. Sensation is a kind of experience: through my power of sight I experience something at first hand and know for myself that it is present; I can speak of it with confidence and clarity; I can knowledgeably invite others to experience it with me, because I know where and what it is. If the obedient, disciplined, and meditative searcher experiences the truths of faith in an analogous way, this would mean that through the power of reason he would 'see' those truths for himself; he could speak of them with confidence and clarity from the store of his own experience; and he could lead others—equally obedient, equally disciplined—along the meditative path by which they too could see the truth for themselves, as if at first hand. I hesitate to put too much weight on this one passage (for nowhere else in his treatises does Anselm speak of experiencing the truths of faith in this way), but the suggestion is instructive, because it captures so much of what is distinctive about Anselm's theological writing. Though faithful to authority, he almost never cites authority: why cite someone else's testimony for a truth that you have been able to see on your own? Other people may have given you the maps, but you have explored the territory for yourself.

Although Anselm's theological approach was (if my suggestion is correct) deeply rooted in and formed by his life as a monk, monks did not typically write in the way Anselm did, and some—most notably his old mentor Lanfranc—disapproved. Anselm sent his first major treatise, the *Monologion*, to Lanfranc (by then archbishop of Canterbury) for his approval, assuring Lanfranc that he would make whatever changes Lanfranc requested and would even destroy the work if he thought it unworthy of publication. We do not have the text of Lanfranc's reply, but it is clear from Anselm's response that Lanfranc was unhappy that the *Monologion* had no citations of Scripture or the church fathers, particularly Augustine. Anselm defended himself: he had not said anything new, anything that couldn't be defended by quoting Scripture or Augustine, but he had wanted to present his own arguments 'as if discovering them for myself'. Anselm made no changes to the work to accommodate Lanfranc, and he never submitted another work for Lanfranc's approval. (He did, however, write a preface dedicating the work to Lanfranc, and the two remained friends.) Even in this first major work, Anselm was going his own way.

He would grow even more independent as the years went by. In his reply to Lanfranc, he protested that he hadn't said anything new, and that he wouldn't have dared to say anything Augustine had not already said. Two decades later he would write that the truths of the faith are so deep, so inexhaustible, that of course not everything that could be said about them has already been said. The territory is vast, and Anselm will now openly acknowledge that he has explored parts of it that no one else had before.

The monastic life that Anselm had chosen was also a communal life. He was not a hermit—he had briefly entertained that possibility before making his profession at Bec—but one of a body of men all dedicated to the same end and helping one another towards that end. Anselm had a remarkable gift for friendship, and in his early letters especially he writes movingly and with great intensity of his love for his brothers. In a letter to Henry, who had taken his vows at Bec in the early 1060s but transferred to another house since that time, Anselm speaks of the longing that absent brothers rightly feel for each other, and he imagines the joy of reunion, whether in this life or the next (see the box entitled 'To Henry, a monk of Bec').

Some writers struggled with the idea that the joys of heaven are somehow communal—what can the fellowship of any human being add to the joy of seeing God face to face?—but Anselm always builds friendship into his picture of the perfect life of heaven. In his consideration of the joys of heaven in chapter 25 of the *Proslogion*, he first invites us to ponder how everything we love, everything we desire as good, is found in God, the source of all good and fount of every blessing. 'What great joy is there where so great a good is present!' he says. But there is still greater joy yet to be considered:

To Henry, a monk of Bec (September 1070 to spring 1073; Letter 5 (i. 5))

To his dearest lord and brother Henry, Brother Anselm sends greetings.

As much as your reputation, most beloved, testifies to me that your manner of life towards all is growing day by day towards nobility of conduct along with devout holiness, so much is the heart of your friend enkindled with a longing to see what he hears of with love, and to enjoy what he loves to hear of. But because I have no doubt that your love for me is like mine for you, I am also certain that you long for me as I long for you. For those whose minds are fused into one by the fire of love are right to grieve if their bodies are separated by the places where they live. Yet because 'whether we live or die, we belong to the Lord' and not to ourselves, we must be more concerned with what the Lord, to whom we belong, is making of us than with what we, who are not our own, want. Let us therefore serve the longing of brotherly charity in such a way that we serve the dominion of his heavenly will. And let us so display the obedience of subjection demanded by his almighty governance that we preserve the affection of love lavished upon us by divine gift. For we will not be able to unite God's ordering with our own well-being any better than by willingly obeying his will in the arrangement of our own affairs. Furthermore, since both of us have brothers present with us whom we love and who love us in return, as we enjoy them with delight governed by reason, let us fit ourselves to enjoy them with reason filled with delight, and let us pray earnestly that someday we will be together with friends both present and absent to enjoy God himself in their company. For when by heavenly mercy we arrive by our various roads at the homeland for which we now sigh, we will rejoice all the more that we have been called back from our diverse places of exile and now come together.

O human heart, O needy heart, heart that has known troubles, that is indeed overwhelmed by troubles: how greatly would you rejoice if you abounded in all these things! Ask your inmost self whether it can even comprehend its joy at such great happiness. And yet surely if someone else whom you loved in every respect as yourself had that same happiness, your joy would be doubled, for you would rejoice no less for him than for yourself. And if two or three or many more had that same happiness, you would rejoice as much for each of them as you would for yourself, if you loved each one as yourself. Therefore, in that perfect charity of countless happy angels and human beings, where no one will love anyone else less than he loves himself, each one will rejoice for each of the others just as he does for himself. If, then, the human heart will scarcely comprehend its own joy from so great a good, how will it be able to contain so many and such great joys?

This address to the human soul, embedded in a larger address to God, is noteworthy for more than its fervour and its embrace of communal life. It is also a striking piece of dialectic. It is an argument: it states premises and draws inferences from them. Even in his prayers—even while arguing that the joys of heaven are beyond our power of comprehension—Anselm is always engaging in dialectic: always making arguments, clarifying terms, proposing and solving apparent contradictions, separating not just the true from the false but also the more complete truth from the less complete.

What distinguishes Anselm from Lanfranc and other 11th-century figures is not that he uses dialectic, but that he uses it so pervasively. Every one of his treatises (even the *Proslogion*, which has the literary form of a prayer) is composed almost entirely of arguments. Dialectic is the tool by which one explores intellectual territory for oneself; it generates the positive content that fills in the gap left by the absence of authoritative quotations so deplored by Lanfranc. Where other writers might use dialectic to clarify, elucidate, or defend theological claims—claims accepted on the basis of Scriptural or patristic authority—Anselm also uses dialectic to establish the truth of those claims. He professes to offer 'necessary reasons' in support of the doctrines of the Trinity, the Incarnation, and the Atonement, arguments that establish the truth of those doctrines 'by reason alone', with no need to appeal to authority. He offers those arguments as 'a pattern for meditating on the reason of faith'—the original title of the *Monologion.*

By 'the reason of faith' (*ratio fidei*) Anselm means

> the intrinsically rational character of Christian doctrines in virtue
> of which they form a coherent and rationally defensible system.
> Christian doctrines are intrinsically rational because they concern
> the nature and activity of God, who is himself supreme reason and
> exhibits supreme wisdom in everything he does. And because
> human beings are rational by nature, we can grasp the reason
> of faith.

The arguments themselves are not the reason of faith: they are a pattern, a template, for meditating on the reason of faith. It requires both dialectical skill and some measure of spiritual discipline to follow the template, but Anselm is confident that those who can follow it will come to see that what is believed on faith is not merely reasonable, not merely true, but beautiful.

The public and ecclesiastical contexts

Anselm was always happiest when he could be both fully a monk and fully a dialectician in this way, but other responsibilities intruded. Lanfranc left Bec in 1063 to become abbot of the newly founded monastery at Caen, and Anselm was elected to succeed him as prior; in 1078 the saintly founder of the Abbey of Bec, Herluin, died, and Anselm was elected abbot. He found his new duties uncongenial, though he carried them out conscientiously and with reasonable success. He even managed to get some writing done: three philosophical dialogues—*On Truth, On Freedom of Choice*, and *On the Fall of the Devil*—written between 1080 and 1086.

Anselm's great gift for friendship served the abbey well, extending its influence, increasing its prestige, and enlarging its possessions. The extensive secular business required by his role—involving money, lands, attendance at court, endless administrative work, and cultivating relationships with wealthy donors—was not to Anselm's taste: it all belonged to 'the world', which he had renounced when he became a monk. And yet it would be wrong to say that his heart wasn't in it. He believed he was doing God's will, and he genuinely loved those who belonged to his ever-widening circle of friends. He was greatly loved in return, even by some unlikely characters. Only one person is 'reported to have hated Anselm in his maturity': William II.

So Anselm had good reason to resist the archbishopric when William first tried to thrust the crozier upon him. Being archbishop of Canterbury would mean even more worldly business threatening to crowd out his central vocation; and if William lived (as he did, for another seven years), it would also mean contending with an 'impetuous cynic' who could not be won by Anselm's love. Yet Anselm came to believe that it was God's will for him to accept, and so he did. This self-surrender, as Anselm thought of it, brought him into the third context that is crucial for understanding his life and (to a lesser degree) his work: the tumultuous relations between church and state.

William wanted to control the church; he wanted the unwavering allegiance of its bishops; he wanted no rival centre of power in England. Anselm had no quarrel in principle with the king's primacy in secular matters, but when it came to spiritual matters he was firm in his resolve that the archbishop of Canterbury be recognized as the head of the church in England and that the church in turn be free to determine its own conduct without lay interference. The inevitable clash between king and archbishop came quickly.

It began with an ugly dispute about money. Shortly after Anselm's consecration the king was strong-arming his vassals for contributions to a military campaign. Anselm was hesitant to give anything: it might have looked as if he had promised the king money in order get himself consecrated as archbishop, and that would be the grave sin of simony, the buying and selling of ecclesiastical office. Nonetheless, Anselm offered £500. At first William accepted, but then one of his advisers (probably William, bishop of Durham) persuaded him to reject the offer and demand more: 'You have honoured him, enriched him, and raised him above all other princes of England, and now, when considering your need, he should give you two thousand pounds or at least one thousand as a thank offering for your munificence'. Anselm repeated his offer of £500 and was astonished when William refused it, angrily. Some months later, when a number of Anselm's bishops urged him to buy the king's friendship by giving him that £500, Anselm refused. The king, he said, should offer his love as freely to him as he offered his devotion to the king. Besides, he no longer had the money to give. He had given away most of it to the poor.

It had long been the custom of new archbishops of Canterbury to travel to Rome to receive the pallium—a white woollen stole symbolizing their archiepiscopal authority—from the pope. Anselm, always keen to uphold the privileges of the see of Canterbury and eager to exercise his authority for the reform and renewal of the church throughout England, wanted to make the customary trip to receive the pallium from Urban II. But William would not allow it. There was a rival claimant to the papacy, Clement III. If Anselm went to Urban, that would in effect commit England to Urban; but only the king, William insisted, had the right to choose between rival popes. Anselm did get his way in the end: envoys from the royal court went secretly to Rome and returned with a papal legate who placed the pallium on the altar at Canterbury Cathedral so that Anselm could take it from there 'as though from the hand of Saint Peter'.

This settlement, in which all parties got something they wanted without compromising anything they considered essential, was reached in May of 1095. For two years there was peace between Anselm and the king. Anselm moved ahead with the construction of the new cathedral at Canterbury, finished his letter *On the Incarnation of the Word*, and began work on his great treatise on the Atonement, *Cur Deus Homo* (*Why a God-man?*). Anselm was eager to hold a council aimed at reforming the church, but every time he raised the idea with the king, William replied that he was too busy 'because of the enemies that surrounded him on all sides'. In April of 1097, William finally came back to England from his newly conquered lands in Normandy, but then he was almost immediately off to invade Wales.

Strange as it may seem, the archbishop of Canterbury had knights of his own, and he was expected to supply fighters for the king's military adventures. Anselm complied, only to have the king charge him with sending men who were poorly trained and ill-equipped for battle. The king's anger was genuine, though the specific complaint about the knights seems to have been a pretext and got quietly dropped. Anselm realized that he would never get the king's cooperation for a council, and he asked for permission to go to Rome to consult with the pope. The king refused and would not back down: Anselm owed him loyalty, and if he broke his oath by leaving the kingdom without the king's permission, he would seize all the lands of the archbishopric and never recognize Anselm as archbishop again. Anselm insisted on going anyway. Before he left, he spoke kindly to William and offered to bless him. Remarkably, the king bowed his head to receive the sign of the Cross. The king and his archbishop would never see each other again.

Anselm was welcomed in Rome, but the papal court moved slowly; while he waited for decisions to be made, he went with

John, formerly a monk of Bec and now abbot of Telese, to stay at the mountaintop retreat of Liberi. There, in early summer of 1098, he was free for a short time to live the simple monastic life he had known in the earliest years of his profession. He was able to write again without distraction, completing *Cur Deus Homo*. Anselm pleaded with the pope to relieve him of the burden of office, but Urban would not allow it. Instead, he had new work for Anselm to do. There was going to be a council at Bari, and the pope wanted Anselm there to defend the Latin doctrine that the Holy Spirit proceeds from the Father and the Son, against the Greek doctrine that the Holy Spirit proceeds only from the Father. Anselm did as he was asked, later writing up his address as the treatise *On the Procession of the Holy Spirit*.

Anselm left Liberi and ended up, after a few months of travel, enjoying the hospitality of the pope in Rome. An envoy from the king arrived, insisting that by leaving England without permission Anselm had knowingly forfeited all his possessions. The pope countered that William would be excommunicated if he did not restore Anselm's possessions and inform the pope of that fact in time for the Roman synod scheduled for April 1099. Some well-judged bribery on the part of the royal envoy secured an extension: Michaelmas (29 September) of that year. Anselm was disgusted and disillusioned by the impotence of the papal court; he would have left Rome immediately, but the pope convinced him to stay for the synod.

It might well have been better for Anselm if he had left right away, because he would hear something at the synod that would further embitter his relationship with the king. At the conclusion of the council the pope pronounced his final excommunications, two of which startled Anselm. The eminent historian R. W. Southern writes:

> The first declared excommunicate all laymen who gave, and all
> clergy who received, lay investiture of churches or ecclesiastical

offices, and any bishop who consecrated a clerk who had been thus invested. The second excommunicated all clergy who did homage to laymen for ecclesiastical possessions, as well as those who associated with them afterwards.

Anselm was shocked and horrified. After all, he had been invested—appointed and given the pastoral staff—by William II, and he had done homage to the king for the possessions of the archdiocese; he had certainly consecrated bishops who had received lay investiture and done such homage. Though the prohibition on lay investiture dated back to 1078 during the papacy of Gregory VII, Anselm had known nothing about it. Lay investiture was business as usual in the Norman and Anglo-Norman church, and suddenly Anselm found that he was in flagrant, if unwitting, violation of papal decrees. What was to be done?

Oddly, instead of remaining in Rome to get counsel from the pope, Anselm left the day after the synod for Lyons. He had been eager enough to leave after the disappointment over William II's delayed excommunication, and perhaps the shock of the papal pronouncements had made the prospect of staying in Rome even more unpleasant. While he stayed with the archbishop of Lyons he composed the last of his devotional writings, the *Meditation on Human Redemption*, which recapitulated the argument of *Cur Deus Homo* in the form of a meditation. He also wrote a treatise *On the Virginal Conception, and On Original Sin*, which took up some questions related to the subject matter of *Cur Deus Homo* that he had not had space to raise in that earlier work.

In August 1100 William II died and was succeeded by his brother Henry I. The new king had no interest in his brother's old grudges against the archbishop—was prepared, in fact, to concede to Anselm everything William had denied him—and pressed Anselm to return to England. Anselm lost no time in setting out, landing in Dover in late September. A few days after his arrival he met with Henry, who asked him to do homage and to receive the archbishopric from him. This was the customary thing to do, so Anselm shocked the king and court when he refused. He reported what he had heard at the synod: there was to be no more lay investiture.

Anselm seems never to have cared about lay investiture one way or the other for its own sake. He never theorized about it; he never sought to understand, let alone to explain, why the prohibition was a salutary instrument for the reform and strengthening of the church. Nowhere in any of his treatises is it ever touched on: a striking instance, one of many, in which Anselm's political context works in isolation from his intellectual context. Yet his monastic ideals of obedience and good order were crucial in the way he carried out his part in the English phase of the investiture controversy. The pope had decreed, and as a matter of conscience Anselm had to obey. If the king would not comply, Anselm said, there could be no peace between them, and he would have to leave England again.

Henry was not the hothead his brother had been. Though he was not prepared to concede what he regarded as an important part of the royal prerogative, he also recognized that his own hold on power was shaky. His brother, Robert Curthose, duke of Normandy, had recently returned from the Crusades with a wife and the wealth that she brought; nobles on both sides of the Channel looked favourably on the idea of reuniting England and Normandy under a single crown. Robert was preparing to invade. A public spat with Anselm would make him look ineffectual; worse, if Anselm decided to favour Robert, the consequences could be even graver.

So Henry was cautious. He agreed to restore Canterbury's lands and refrain from investing any bishop or abbot. He would send envoys to Pope Paschal II (Urban having died in 1099) asking for permission for England to maintain its traditional customs rather than following the new decrees about investiture; Anselm sent a letter along with them, asking the pope to grant the king's request. In the meantime Henry and Anselm worked closely and productively together. When Robert invaded England in 1101, Henry had Anselm's public support, even relying on Anselm to persuade magnates whose loyalty was in question. And Anselm was at last allowed to hold his long-desired primatial council in London in September 1102.

Pope Paschal refused the dispensation for which Henry and Anselm had asked. He did make a veiled offer of papal support for Henry's claim to the throne of England against Robert in exchange for Henry's compliance with the prohibition on lay investiture, but by the time the letter arrived there was no need: Henry had defeated Robert and received his recognition as king. His hold on power now consolidated, Henry could afford to be more forthright in his demands. He summoned Anselm to court in September 1101 and gave him an ultimatum: either Anselm would agree to defy the pope, do homage, and consecrate the bishops and abbot who had received royal investiture, or he must leave England.

Anselm did neither. He patiently explained his position, made whatever compromise he could in good conscience make, and encouraged both the king and the pope to greater flexibility. Neither Paschal nor Henry was open to compromise, but Henry was at least open to one last attempt to resolve the impasse. With the unanimous backing of his magnates and prelates, Henry persuaded Anselm to go in person to the pope along with the king's own experienced papal negotiator, William Warelwast, to ask for the dispensation that both king and archbishop wanted. But the pope would not budge, and only after that final refusal did Anselm learn of Henry's back-up plan: William informed him that if he did not agree to lay investiture, he was not welcome to return to England.

Anselm's exile lasted from December 1103 until August 1106. Henry eventually succumbed to Anselm's threat of excommunication, coming in the midst of some political reversals that made him vulnerable once again, and agreed to a compromise: he would give up lay investiture if he could retain homage from bishops and abbots. The pope accepted the compromise, and Anselm returned to England at the king's urging in August 1106.

Anselm was well into his seventies by that point, and he was growing physically weak, though his mind was as sharp as ever and he was energetic in his work as archbishop. He finished one last treatise, *On the Harmony of God's Foreknowledge, Predestination, and Grace with Free Choice*, as remarkable a piece of dialectic as anything he ever wrote. He had another work planned: he told his monks that he had been devoting a great deal of thought to the origin of the soul—a matter that Augustine had famously left unresolved—and would be glad if he might be spared to write it, 'because I do not know if anyone else will be able to provide a solution after I am gone'. But by then his final illness was upon him, and the treatise on the origin of the soul was left unwritten. Anselm died as dawn was breaking on the Wednesday of Holy Week, 21 April 1109, 'with the whole congregation of his sons gathered around him'.

Chapter 2
Looking at God

Textbooks in the philosophy of religion often put their section on
arguments for the existence of God before their section on the
nature and attributes of God. It takes only a moment's reflection
to see that this gets the order backward. I can't pronounce on the
existence of unicorns unless I first know what unicorns are—or,
rather, what unicorns would be if there were any—and I can't
expound or evaluate an argument for the existence of God unless
I have first worked out what something would have to be in order
to count as God. I need something like a mental sketch of the
being and nature of God before I have any hope of determining
whether the original of that sketch genuinely exists in the world
outside my mind. I examine this sketch and then try to find
arguments that show there is a real being who matches it. In the
terms I've used for the titles of this chapter and the next, first
I look *at* God, then I look *for* God.

Anselm's aim and audience

Anselm carries out both projects, the looking-at and the looking-for,
most extensively in two of his earliest treatises, the *Monologion*
(1075–6) and the *Proslogion* (1077–8), but the concept of God he
develops there remains consistent throughout his career. In
neither work does he pretend to be developing an account of the
divine nature from scratch: the God he is looking at and looking

for is explicitly the God of Christian belief. In the *Monologion* he describes the being in question as 'one nature, supreme among all existing things, who alone is self-sufficient in his eternal happiness, who through his omnipotent goodness grants and brings it about that all other things exist or have any sort of well-being', and of whom 'many other things that we [Christians] must believe about God' are true. But although the description of God is to some extent fixed by revelation (refined, as we shall see, through philosophy), the arguments that there is such a being are meant to be purely rational. The *Monologion* is presented as a template for meditation on God by which readers can 'convince themselves of most of these things by reason alone, if they are even moderately intelligent'.

The *Proslogion* has a very different literary form, but a similar aim. It is not a treatise but a prayer, beginning with an anguished and urgent address to a God who seems bewilderingly, enticingly hidden:

> Let me look up at your light, whether from afar or from the depths.
> Teach me how to seek you, and show yourself to me when I seek.
> For I cannot seek you unless you teach me how, and I cannot find
> you unless you show yourself to me. Let me seek you in desiring
> you; let me desire you in seeking you. Let me find you in loving you;
> let me love you in finding you.

It is a speech that only a believer could make, and Anselm goes on to specify that what he seeks is precisely to understand what he already believes:

> Therefore, Lord, you who grant understanding to faith, grant that,
> insofar as you know it is useful for me, I may understand that you
> exist as we believe you exist, and that you are what we believe
> you to be.

Still, although faith—broadly understood to include Holy Scripture, the teachings of the church, and the texts of the church fathers, among whom Augustine is paramount—supplies at least the outlines of the sketch of God that Anselm will be drawing, he is confident that both his sketch of the divine nature and his arguments for God's existence have rational force that should in principle be convincing to anyone. The 'moderately intelligent' people who can use the arguments of the *Monologion* to convince themselves of the truths of faith are explicitly described as those who either do not believe or have never heard of those truths, and the argument of the *Proslogion* is intended to convince the Psalmist's fool, who 'has said in his heart, "There is no God"'.

How to think God

And what do Christians believe about God? Anselm's most famous and most useful formulation comes in the *Proslogion*, where he says, 'We believe that you are something than which nothing greater can be thought'. That is, God is so great that we cannot even think something greater than God. God is not merely a being who happens to be unsurpassed in greatness, but a being who is unsurpassable in greatness. If we are thinking a being that is not the greatest possible being, we are not managing to think God.

Now this definition or characterization of God includes at least two terms that need further definition themselves: what does Anselm mean by greatness, and what does Anselm mean when he speaks of 'thinking' something? I deliberately use 'think' without the 'of' that normally accompanies it in contemporary English to emphasize that Anselm has a particular account of thought in mind, one in which the things we think are the direct objects of our act of thinking. To think something is to get it before one's mind. We can think things more or less accurately, more or less precisely, so thinking need not be a matter of fully understanding or completely comprehending a thing. (We cannot completely comprehend God, as it will turn out.) It is a matter of having the thing in our mental gaze, so to speak. This we can do by imagining something, by entertaining the concept of its essence or nature, by formulating a description that distinguishes it from other things: there is no single way that thinking has to work.

Objects of thought include not only real things, such as horses and lakes, but also imaginary things, such as unicorns and fauns, and even unrealized possibilities, such as my older brother Jason. All of these are objects of thought—that is, we can get any of these objects before the gaze of our minds—whether they exist in the world outside the mind or not. We cannot, however, think impossibilities. Square circles and surfaces that are both red all over and green all over are not objects of thought: we can say those words, we can write them down or rehearse them in our heads, but there is no corresponding object to get before our minds. So we can think things that don't exist, never have existed, and never will exist; but we cannot think things that cannot exist.

This account of thinking, which Anselm works out in the *Monologion*, means that thinking God is not a mere matter of using a verbal formula—'that than which a greater cannot be thought'—and doing logical moves with it. Thinking God means actually getting God before one's mind, having a thought about God that does not, as it were, 'misfire'. In order to do this, we must perform a fair bit of preliminary intellectual work, which Anselm describes as 'forming an idea of God'. We can begin that work by exploring the second key concept in Anselm's *Proslogion* description of God: greatness.

'I do not mean great in size', Anselm explains; instead he has in mind the sense of greatness in which 'the greater something is, the better or worthier it is, as wisdom is great'. To form our idea of God, we need to work out systematically what characteristics a thing would have to have in order to be so great that it is impossible to think a greater being. Some of the familiar divine attributes come immediately to mind: it is clearly greater to be unlimited in knowledge than to be limited in knowledge, greater to be unlimited in power than to be limited in power, so anything that would count as God must be omniscient and omnipotent. Other divine attributes are more obvious against the background of a particular philosophical and theological tradition that goes back through Augustine to Greek thought. According to that tradition, the eternal is greater than the temporal, the immaterial than the material, the immutable than the mutable. God must, therefore, be eternal, immutable, and immaterial.

God's nature: eternal, immutable, immaterial

Divine eternity is not a matter of God's existing at every time, but rather of God's existing outside time altogether. Existence in time is a limitation: one moment succeeds another, present experience is constantly slipping away into the past, and the life of a temporal being is confined to a tiny sliver of a fleeting 'now'. The life of an eternal being, by contrast, is complete all at once: it has no past that has slipped away, no future possessed only in anticipation, only a 'now' that, unlike ours, is not fleeting, but abides without gain or loss. Clearly, then, it is greater to be eternal than to be temporal, so we know that God is eternal. And an eternal being must necessarily also be an immutable being, since change requires a before and after, and there is no before and after in the life of an eternal being.

Similar considerations show that it is greater to be immaterial than material. Material objects are extended; they are made up of parts and can therefore be broken apart, at least in thought if not in reality, fragmented in place just as temporal beings are fragmented in time:

> This, then, is the condition of place and time: whatever is enclosed within their boundaries does not escape being characterized by parts, whether the sort of parts its place receives with respect to

size, or the sort its time suffers with respect to duration; nor can it in any way be contained as a whole all at once by different places or times. By contrast, if something is in no way constrained by confinement in a place or time, no law of places or times forces it into a multiplicity of parts or prevents it from being present as a whole all at once in several places or times. And so, since this is the condition of place and time, the supreme substance, who is not enclosed by any confinement of place or time, is undoubtedly not constrained by any of their laws.

Notice that Anselm does not simply treat it as intuitively obvious that the eternal is greater than the temporal and the immaterial than the material, well-entrenched though those claims were in the tradition to which he belonged. In this passage he offers reasons for those judgements. To be temporal, to be material, is to be enclosed and constrained; what is eternal and immaterial is unbounded and unconstrained. Most important, what is temporal and material is fragmented and multiple; what is eternal and immaterial is a unity.

God's nature: simplicity and aseity

The claim that God has no parts of any kind, but instead is an indivisible unity, is known as the doctrine of divine simplicity. We have seen that God has no temporal or material parts, but divine simplicity also means that God has no metaphysical parts. That is, God does not have multiple attributes; nor is there any distinction between God and his attributes. Ordinary objects are metaphysically composite: I have various features, such as nearsightedness and baldness, and those features are distinct from each other (nearsightedness is not baldness) and distinct from me (I could, and indeed once did, exist without either of them). But God's omnipotence is not distinct from God's omniscience, and neither God's omnipotence nor God's omniscience is distinct from God. God's omniscience is the very same thing as God's omnipotence, which is the very same thing as God. And so on for all the other divine attributes (to continue speaking illegitimately of 'attributes' in the plural): God's wisdom = God's love = God's eternity = God's power = God's justice = God.

Divine simplicity is such a counterintuitive doctrine that it is worth looking carefully at why Anselm is committed to it. Why does unsurpassable greatness require a lack of metaphysical composition? One argument Anselm gives is that any composite can be broken up, at least in thought, and clearly what can be broken up is inferior to what cannot be broken up. This argument might well seem like a mere restatement of the general preference for unity over multiplicity, and so it might be less than convincing to someone who doesn't quite see why divine unity has to be (or even intelligibly can be) carried quite so far as to deny any metaphysical distinctions in God.

Anselm has a more powerful consideration available, however, in what philosophers nowadays call divine *aseity*. 'Aseity' is derived from the Latin *a se*, 'from himself' (though no medieval philosopher writing in Latin actually uses the word *aseitas*—it is odd that it was left to later writers to coin a faux-Latin word for a concept that was so important to medieval Latin writers). The idea is that whatever God is, he is from himself. He does not depend on anything outside himself to be what he is. Now it is easy to see why aseity must characterize a being of unsurpassable greatness: it is greater, better, nobler to be independent than dependent, to have in oneself the fount and source of all that one is, rather than depending on something outside oneself to exist or to be what one is.

Once we understand aseity, it is easy to see why God cannot be a composite in any way. A composite depends on its components if it is to exist and to be what it is. If God has parts—attributes distinct from each other or from God himself—then he depends on something other than himself to be what he is. So God does not *have* wisdom or power or justice; God *is* wisdom and power and justice, which are all one in God, because they *are* God, and God is one.

God's nature: omnipotence

Although Anselm accepts the claim that God is simple in this very strong sense, he generally proceeds by analysing individual divine attributes separately. (One could hardly do otherwise.) I have already discussed Anselm's account of divine eternity, but other attributes I have already mentioned, as well as some I have yet to introduce, receive sustained attention in Anselm's works. Divine omnipotence famously generates puzzles and paradoxes. Anselm asks how God can be omnipotent when there are things God cannot do. God cannot lie, for example: his perfect goodness prohibits it. The answer is that omnipotence does not mean the ability to do everything; it means the possession of all power. We might say that I have the 'ability' or 'power' to lie, or even simply that I 'can' lie, but all those expressions are misleading. This so-called ability is really a weakness: it is a liability to moral corruption, a limitation on my power to hold on to the truth. God is in no way liable to corruption, and his power is in no way limited. Consequently, God's 'inability' to lie is not a constraint on his omnipotence, but a consequence of his omnipotence. To put it another way, God's omnipotence does not mean that every sentence beginning with 'God can' will turn out to be true, because we sometimes use 'can' (and related words) improperly. Only when the 'can' genuinely expresses power rather than weakness or limitation will it be true to say that 'God can' do whatever it is.

Anselm did not know the paradox of the stone, but his account offers an elegant resolution of the paradox nonetheless. The paradox of the stone is meant to show that the notion of omnipotence is incoherent. Can God make a stone so heavy that even he cannot lift it? If you answer yes, there's something God cannot do: he can't lift the stone. If you answer no, there's something God cannot do: he can't make the stone. So either way, there's something God cannot do; God is not omnipotent, and indeed no being could be. To this Anselm would certainly reply that the 'power' to create something that can escape one's own control is no power at all, but a weakness. God has unlimited power to create and unlimited power to control.

God's nature: omniscience

Omniscience poses difficulties that cannot be so easily resolved by clarifying our ordinary language. That God must be omniscient seems clear enough: God's knowledge must be unlimited, because it is greater to have unlimited knowledge than to be limited in one's knowledge. Ignorance is both a metaphysical limitation and a moral liability, and we cannot suppose that God suffers from either kind of deficiency. So God's knowledge encompasses everything there is to know. Yet God is supposed to be eternal—there is no before and after in God, only a timeless 'now'—whereas things other than God are in time. They are changing, fleeting, existing in a 'now' that itself exists only by slipping away into nothingness. It would seem that to know something that is undergoing change, God would himself have to undergo change: first he knows that I am typing this sentence, then he knows that I am typing the next sentence. Yet there can be no 'first' and 'then' in God.

To make matters more complicated, Anselm takes it for granted that God's boundless knowledge includes complete knowledge of the future (our future, of course: God has no future). But God's knowledge, being eternal, is fixed and immutable, whereas we at least like to think that the future is open. Suppose tomorrow I am faced with a choice: I can either tell a difficult and uncomfortable truth or else fall back on a convenient lie. If my choice is free, then both options are open to me; as long as that choice is in the future, it is not fixed or determinate. Only when I have made the choice is it fixed in the way that all past things are fixed. So divine foreknowledge requires that what is foreknown is fixed and immutable, but freedom requires that free actions are unfixed and open until they are actually made.

In his famous discussion of divine eternity, freedom, and foreknowledge in Book V of *The Consolation of Philosophy*, Boethius had proposed a model for thinking about these matters. According to Boethius, we should think about God's eternal vantage point in something like the way we think about watching a race from high up in the stands. Just as the whole track is spread out before our vision, the whole of time is spread out before God's mind; he takes it all in at once. So God can and does know what is taking place in time, because he sees the whole of time in one glance. He even knows our free actions because he sees them taking place, but that knowledge doesn't threaten their status as free, because it imposes no necessity or fixity on them, any more than my seeing one runner overtake another imposes some sort of necessity on the runner. It doesn't happen because I see it; I see it because it happens.

Influential though Boethius's discussion was, Anselm cannot accept it. First, on Anselm's view, time really does flow; there is an ever-changing 'now'. So there simply is no 'whole of time' that can be spread out for a God's-eye view to take in all at once. Second, and worse, Boethius's account of foreknowledge is incompatible with divine aseity. God can't derive his knowledge from things, because he would then depend on things outside himself to be what he is, omniscient. Instead, Anselm says, things derive from God's knowledge.

In saying that things derive from God's knowledge, Anselm is insisting on an important tenet of classical theism that for some reason does not have a name of its own, so I have taken to calling it 'divine ultimacy'. Divine ultimacy is the flip side of divine aseity: just as divine aseity means that God depends on nothing other than himself to be what he is, divine ultimacy means that everything other than God depends on God to be what it is. Anselm takes divine ultimacy with particular seriousness. No place, no time, no action, no choice, no being of any sort can exist apart from God's sustaining presence. Whatever has being derives

28

that being from God, not just initially, but at every moment of its existence. So, when Anselm says that things derive from God's knowledge, he is expressing what he takes to be an obvious consequence of divine ultimacy. God knows what he brings about, and what he brings about is everything other than himself.

An objection arises immediately. Does this not mean that God is 'the culprit and instigator in all evil deeds'? No, Anselm says, because the evil of evil deeds is precisely nothing. It has no being; it is a lack of goodness where goodness ought to be. Anselm takes over this account (known as the privation theory of evil) from Augustine, who had put it to a similar use. Anselm argues in various places that moral evil, injustice, can exist only in the will of a rational being—an angel or human being—and that such injustice is purely a privation, a lack of the justice that should be present in the will. Here he argues that since the injustice of an evil will is not a being, but a lack of being, we can consistently say both that God brings about all that has being and that God does not bring about evil deeds.

The privation theory of evil offers a ready-made solution to the problem of defending divine aseity and ultimacy without implicating God in moral evil. The problem of reconciling the fixity of God's foreknowledge with the openness of free choices requires a more innovative solution. Anselm adopts what we might call a 'dual presentism'. In contemporary philosophy, presentism is the view that only what exists now is real; the past no longer exists, the future does not yet exist. All that there is of time—all that there is of reality—is the ever-flowing now and whatever exists in that now. Contrast this with the picture we get on Boethius's view, on which all of time is equally real. On such a view, which contemporary philosophers call 'eternalism', there is no privileged now, much as in space there is no privileged here. If I am in Edinburgh, Tampa is not here, but it is equally real; similarly, says the eternalist, if I am in 2022, 1967 is not now, but it is equally real.

Anselm takes the presentist view about time and sets alongside it a presentist view about eternity. Just as the present has its now—ever-flowing, always slipping away into the unreality of the past—eternity also has its now. Only what exists now exists, but the now of eternity encompasses everything. So we have two presents, two nows, irreducibly distinct from each other. If I ask, then, 'Does my free choice tomorrow about whether to lie exist now?', there is no single answer to the question. If the question is asking about the now of time, then no, clearly, because tomorrow does not exist now. If the question is asking about the now of eternity, then yes. Similarly, if I ask whether that choice is open or fixed, there is no single answer to the question. In time my choice is open; in eternity it is fixed.

This solution to the problem of freedom and foreknowledge is offered in the last of Anselm's completed works, *De concordia*. (Its full title is *De concordia praescientiae et praedestinationis et gratiae Dei cum libero arbitrio*, or *On the Harmony of God's Foreknowledge, Predestination, and Grace with Free Choice*, but it is invariably just called *De concordia*.) One striking feature of the solution is that it relies entirely on theses Anselm had argued for and developed already: the nature of time and eternity, their relationship, even the claim that one and the same question can have different answers when asked from different perspectives. In a way there is nothing new here, just a brilliant and creative application of things Anselm had already said. If Anselm hadn't written *De concordia*, we might even try to apply those earlier claims ourselves to work out how Anselm might have addressed the problem. (For a brief discussion of the pitfalls of doing that sort of thing, see the box entitled 'A word about methodology in interpreting Anselm'.)

God's nature: impassibility, justice, and mercy

By this point in our examination of Anselm's portrait (surely more than a sketch by now) of the divine nature, perhaps you have begun to notice how frequently one divine attribute implies another. Though we think God using a number of different concepts, those concepts fit together in such a way that it really is correct to speak of *the* account of God that emerges. Aseity implies simplicity; simplicity implies eternity; eternity implies immutability. (All those implications work in the reverse direction as well, if you think about it.) The next important divine attribute to be considered is so closely connected with aseity, simplicity, eternity, and immutability that it arguably follows from any of the four. I am speaking of divine impassibility. That God is impassible means that he does not experience any emotions. Emotions are things we undergo, rather than things we do, so aseity rules them out in God's case. They are distinct from the person who undergoes them, contrary to divine simplicity. Finally, they involve physical change, contrary to both simplicity (God has no physical parts) and immutability (God cannot undergo change of any kind). The idea that God is impassible is so firmly entrenched in the Augustinian tradition that Anselm does not even feel the need to argue for it.

Strikingly, though, he does feel the need to defend it. In the two places where he talks about divine impassibility (the word *impassibilis* appears just eight times in the treatises), he talks about it as a problem for the consistency of our view of God. In the more extensive discussion in the *Proslogion*, Anselm asks how divine impassibility can be compatible with divine mercy. To be merciful (*misericors*), Anselm proposes, is to have a sorrowful heart (*miserum cor*); it is to share in someone else's suffering (*compati*, the noun form of which is *compassio*). But God cannot suffer; he cannot feel sorrow. How, then, can he be merciful? Anselm answers that God is merciful without feeling. We feel the *effect* of God's mercy—our punishment is lightened, perhaps, or our sorrow relieved—but God does not feel the *affect* of mercy. He is not 'afflicted with any feeling of compassion for sorrow'.

Mercy presents another difficulty. We know that God is merciful, not only by the abundant testimony of Scripture but on philosophical grounds, since 'it is better to be merciful than not to be merciful'. Yet we also know—and from the same sources—that God is supremely just. Surely, however, God's justice means that he rewards the good and punishes the wicked. Yet God's mercy means that he spares the wicked. How, then, can God be both just and merciful?

Anselm devotes three chapters of the *Proslogion* to this conundrum, making some headway on the question but ultimately leaving it unresolved. He begins by rooting divine mercy in divine goodness:

You would be less good if you were not kind to any wicked person. For one who is good both to the good and to the wicked is better than one who is good only to the good, and one who is good to the wicked both in punishing and in sparing them is better than one who is good only in punishing them. So it follows that you are merciful precisely because you are totally and supremely good.

This conclusion is certainly helpful, Anselm thinks—and he proceeds to elaborate it in two paragraphs of praise to God for his goodness—but it might also seem to have simply relocated the original problem. Instead of an apparent conflict between justice and mercy, we now have an apparent conflict between justice and goodness.

But we know that 'there is no goodness apart from justice—indeed, goodness is actually in harmony with justice', so we must see how goodness and justice harmonize in God's treatment of the wicked. Anselm first suggests that when God punishes the wicked, he is just towards them: he is giving them the punishment they deserve. But when God spares the wicked, he is just towards himself: he is giving his supreme goodness the appropriate scope. In other words, when God punishes the wicked, he gives them their due; when he spares the wicked, he gives himself his due.

Yet we must also say that God gives himself his due when he punishes the wicked: 'It is certainly just for you to be so just that you cannot be thought to be more just. And you would by no means be so just if you only repaid the good with good and did not repay the wicked with evil'. At this point Anselm reaches the end of what logical analysis can do. We can understand how divine justice is manifest both in punishing and in sparing the wicked, but why are certain wicked people condemned and others, 'alike in wickedness', spared? We simply cannot know.

It is uncharacteristic of Anselm to bring us to the brink of mystery and then leave us there; he is constitutionally averse to leaving intellectual loose ends dangling. That he does so here in his discussion of divine mercy and justice could be interpreted in two ways (which are not mutually exclusive). First, Anselm says that it is a matter for God's will to decide whom he will condemn and whom he will spare, and he may well think that there is no explanation for why God wills as he does in particular cases. Such an explanation might have to point to something that causes or constrains God in some way, contrary to divine aseity. If this is Anselm's view, then the mystery is not that we cannot know the reason God chooses one way rather than the other; it's that there is simply no such reason to be known.

A second interpretation is that Anselm thinks the last word on divine justice and mercy needs to be said, not in these abstract considerations about the divine nature, but rather in his account of the divine plan of redemption. In that account we obtain a fuller view of God's purposes in creation, human destiny, and the extraordinary mechanism by which God acts to reconcile human beings with himself. We will return, then, to the mercy and justice of God when we examine the great restoration project in Chapter 6.

Chapter 3
Looking for God

Anselm probably never met a professed atheist. He knew non-Christians, certainly: formidable objections to the Christian account of redemption raised by some learned Jews recently arrived in London were a key impetus to his treatise on the Atonement (*Cur Deus Homo*, 1094–8). But complete unbelief was something he knew as a possibility only from Scripture: 'The fool has said in his heart, "There is no God"'. Yet he took seriously the challenge of proving that there is a God, and that God is what Christians believe he is. Why?

Faith seeking understanding

It was not because unbelief was a live option, for him or for anyone he knew, but because he longed to understand what he believed. We owe to Anselm the phrase 'faith seeking understanding', which was the original title of the *Proslogion*, in which he set forth his most famous argument for the existence of God. We entirely miss the point of faith seeking understanding if we think of it purely as a matter of intellectual restlessness: I believe x, but I won't feel as though my belief in x is intellectually respectable until I can offer a proof that x is true. The enterprise is at least as much a matter of love as it is of knowledge. I love the truth, and in faith I glimpse it, but only partially, fleetingly. I want to rest in it, luxuriate in it, possess it fully instead of merely yearning for it.

Anselm's arguments for the existence of God are efforts to possess the truth of God's existence and nature as fully as possible. They begin with faith, in the sense that the motivation for engaging in the arguments is the lively desire to know in full what at first one only glimpses in part. But the arguments are meant to be persuasive, at least in principle, even to the unbeliever: for if I cannot put the existence and nature of God beyond the range of all scruple and doubt, how can I rest in it as something fully known?

Two ways of looking for God

In the terms I have been using thus far, once we have our sketch of God—our account of what a thing would have to be in order to count as God—we look for arguments to show that there is something in the real world that matches the sketch, something real that answers to the description we have developed. There are basically two ways to go about doing this: one can try to find features of the world that can only be explained (or can best be explained) by the existence of a being that matches the sketch, or one can look for features in the sketch itself that guarantee that the original of the sketch must exist.

The first way is by far the more common; nearly all of the arguments for the existence of God discussed in philosophy, or debated in popular culture, are of this general form. Consider the following, which are very compressed versions of commonly discussed arguments:

• The universe exhibits features that can only be explained by positing an intelligent Mind with enough power to create and order the whole universe.

- Whatever is in motion must be moved by something else. But there cannot be an infinite regress of movers, so we must posit a First Unmoved Mover.

- Contingent things—things that can either exist or not exist—are not self-explaining. They do not contain in themselves the reason for their existence. But everything has an ultimate and sufficient explanation, and that can only be a self-explaining being: a necessary being (one that cannot fail to exist) whose very nature explains its existence.

Anselm develops a few versions of this kind of argument in the *Monologion*. In chapter 1, for example, he begins from the observation that we encounter a variety of good things, some better than others. The goodness of those good things is the same goodness in each of them: there is more goodness in some than in others, but what goodness itself is does not vary. The goodness through which all good things are good must itself be a very great good, precisely because all good things exist through it. But if goodness itself is a great good, and all goods are good through it, it follows that goodness is good through itself. All other good things are good derivatively; goodness itself is non-derivatively good, and therefore supremely good.

This argument, assuming that it's successful, establishes the existence of something supremely good. But now compare that result to the sketch of God Anselm has developed, and the result looks very meagre. Is this supremely good thing omnipotent or omniscient? Does it have a mind and will, so that it can be just and merciful? The argument doesn't tell us; we'll need further arguments to establish the existence of something close enough to our sketch to justify identifying it as God. Anselm is aware of this, and he goes on in the *Monologion* to develop those further arguments. But he comes to be dissatisfied, not with any of those arguments in particular, but with the fact that the *Monologion* was 'constructed out of a chaining together of many arguments'.

What he wanted was a single argument that would do everything at once: one argument that 'would by itself be enough to show that God really exists...and whatever we believe about the divine nature'. He became obsessed with the struggle to find this single argument: sometimes success felt just out of reach, sometimes the whole project seemed hopeless. The thought hounded him, try as he might to banish it; he lost his appetite, couldn't sleep, and was too distracted to pay attention during the Daily Office—surely a sign that the whole enterprise was a temptation from the devil. At last, however, the argument came to him (during the Daily Office).

The single argument

The distinctive feature of this new argument was that it worked in the second way I mentioned earlier: by looking directly at the sketch of God and identifying features in that sketch that guarantee that the being depicted in it must exist in reality. This approach eliminates any need for a long string of arguments proving a variety of distinct conclusions about God, because a full account of the divine nature is already laid out in the sketch; if the argument shows that the original of the sketch exists, it automatically shows that there is a real being with all the features of the divine nature. This is how it can function as 'one argument', just as Anselm wanted.

Arguments of this type, which move from the idea of God to the existence of God, are called ontological arguments; Anselm's 'one argument' is the first ontological argument. It has proved both endlessly fascinating and endlessly controversial: it has been defended, demolished, and rehabilitated again and again over the years. As with any significant philosophical argument, there is no consensus about whether it succeeds or fails (and, if it fails, how).

Unlike many other significant arguments, however, there is no consensus even about what the argument *is*. We can start, however, with a reasonably popular mainstream reading of the argument—more or less the reading you would find in philosophy of religion textbooks or get taught in an introduction to philosophy class—before looking at what I think is a more faithful reading.

It is best to have the text of the argument in front of us: I give the full text of *Proslogion* 2 in the box entitled '*Proslogion* 2, the ontological argument'.

In an ontological argument, as I have said, we start with a portrait of God and then argue that some feature of that portrait implies the real existence of God. The portrait of God in this passage is clearly the description 'that than which a greater cannot be thought', the full meaning of which we explored in Chapter 2. It seems perfectly possible, Anselm acknowledges, to doubt whether there is any actual being that corresponds to that description. After all, 'The fool has said in his heart, "There is no God"'. But we can convince the fool that he is wrong just by getting him to think through the implications of 'that than which a greater cannot be thought'. The fool does at least understand that definition. Now whatever is understood exists in the understanding, just as the plan of a painting she has yet to execute already exists in the understanding of the painter. So that than which a greater cannot be thought exists in the understanding (even the fool's understanding). But if it exists in the understanding, it must also exist in reality. For it is greater to exist in reality than to exist merely in the understanding. Therefore, if that than which a greater cannot be thought existed only in the understanding, it would be possible to think something greater than it (namely, that same being existing in reality as well). It follows, then, that if that than which a greater cannot be thought existed only in the understanding, it would not be that than which a greater cannot be thought; and that, obviously, is a contradiction. So that than which a greater cannot be thought must exist in reality, not merely in the understanding.

Proslogion 2, the ontological argument

Therefore, Lord, you who grant understanding to faith, grant that, insofar as you know it is useful for me, I may understand that you exist as we believe you exist, and that you are what we believe you to be. Now we believe that you are something than which nothing greater can be thought. So can it be that no such nature exists, since 'The fool has said in his heart, "There is no God"'? But when this same fool hears me say 'something than which nothing greater can be thought', he surely understands what he hears; and what he understands exists in his understanding, even if he does not understand that it exists [in reality]. For it is one thing for an object to exist in the understanding and quite another to understand that the object exists [in reality]. When a painter, for example, thinks out in advance what she is going to paint, she has it in her understanding, but she does not yet understand that it exists, since she has not yet painted it. But once she has painted it, she both has it in her understanding and understands that it exists because she has now painted it. So even the fool must admit that something than which nothing greater can be thought exists at least in his understanding, since he understands this when he hears it, and whatever is understood exists in the understanding. And surely that than which a greater cannot be thought cannot exist only in the understanding. For if it exists only in the understanding, it can be thought to exist in reality as well, which is greater. So if that than which a greater cannot be thought exists only in the understanding, then the very thing than which a greater *cannot* be thought is something than which a greater *can* be thought. But that is clearly impossible. Therefore, there is no doubt that something than which a greater cannot be thought exists both in the understanding and in reality.

Anselm

Gaunilo's rebuttal

The argument attracted criticism almost immediately. An otherwise unknown monk named Gaunilo wrote a rebuttal he entitled 'A Reply on Behalf of the Fool', arguing that Anselm's reasoning should not convince the Psalmist's fool, or indeed anyone else, that God exists. Although he raises a number of criticisms, by far his most striking objection is a parody of Anselm's argument, using the same basic argument to support what is obviously an absurd conclusion. Imagine, Gaunilo says, an island 'more plentifully endowed than even the Isles of the Blessed with an indescribable abundance of all sorts of riches and delights'—an island than which no greater can be thought. I clearly understand this story; there's nothing difficult about it. So by your reasoning, Anselm, that island must exist in reality. Why? Because it is greater to exist in reality than to exist only in the understanding, so if the island does not exist in reality, we can think of an island that would be even greater; but (so your argument goes) we cannot think of an island that is greater than the island than which no greater can be thought. Therefore, the greatest conceivable island exists in reality.

Clearly, Gaunilo says, it would be foolish to believe in the existence of this 'Lost Island' on the basis of such an argument. (And, though Gaunilo does not note this explicitly, there is nothing special about islands. You could use this same form of reasoning to generate proofs of the cockroach than which no greater can be thought, the most excellent oak tree conceivable, and so forth.) So something has gone wrong with Anselm's argument. Though the Lost Island parody by itself doesn't show where the argument fails, Gaunilo strongly suggests that the culprit is the premise that it is greater to exist in reality than in the understanding alone. (For a discussion of that premise, see the box entitled 'Is existence a perfection?'.)

Is existence a perfection?

On my interpretation of Anselm's argument, it will turn out that Anselm doesn't actually rely on the premise that existence is a perfection; but the discussion of this premise is such a traditional part of accounts of Anselm that I feel bound not to pass over it in silence. The standard objection to this premise is expressed in Kant's slogan that 'exists is not a predicate' or 'existence is not a perfection'. The idea is that, contrary to the assumption Gaunilo thinks Anselm is making, existence in reality is not greater than existence in the understanding. Existence is not like wisdom or good looks or the ability to play the piano; it's not a feature that makes a thing better than it would otherwise be.

To see why someone would take this objection seriously, imagine this scenario (which I adapt from the American philosopher Norman Malcolm). Suppose there is a vacancy on the Supreme Court, and the president of the United States sends two of his advisers into separate rooms with instructions to make a list of all the qualities that the best possible nominee will have. After an hour, the advisers return with their lists. Adviser A lists such qualifications as 'has at least three years' experience on a federal appeals court, has judicial philosophy x, has particular expertise in y', and so forth. Adviser B presents the *exact same list* except that at the end, she has written 'exists'. Has Adviser B described a better nominee than Adviser A? Clearly not: she has described exactly the same nominee, only with an eccentric and irrelevant flourish at the end. A nominee who doesn't exist won't have any of the other desirable qualities either.

Anselm was grateful for Gaunilo's spirited engagement with his work (so Eadmer tells us) and wrote a reply, directing that both Gaunilo's criticism and his own response always be appended to the *Proslogion*. In this directive he has been only partly successful. Published translations of the *Proslogion* almost invariably include the exchange with Gaunilo, and Gaunilo's reply gets a lot of attention (the Lost Island parody may well be the most famous counterexample in the history of philosophy), but Anselm's response is less carefully studied. One strangely overlooked point is that Anselm denies ever having used the premise that existence in reality is greater than existence in the understanding alone. Since that is an essential premise both in the standard reading of Anselm's argument and in Gaunilo's parody, the fact that Anselm denies having used that premise—and writes a very long response to Gaunilo, restating his own argument in several different ways, without ever using the premise—should make us suspect that the standard reading is mistaken and that Gaunilo's parody attacks an argument different from the one Anselm took himself to be giving.

Anselm's reply

At the beginning of his reply to Gaunilo, Anselm summarizes what he takes to be Gaunilo's two main criticisms. First, it is not actually possible to think that than which a greater cannot be thought: we can say the words, but the being itself eludes our capacity to paint the mental portrait of God that Anselm claims we have. We'll call this the *unthinkability objection*. Second, even if we *could* think that being, we would not be entitled to conclude that the being exists in reality, outside the mind; we can think any number of beings that don't exist, so what's so special about this one? Because Gaunilo describes thoughts of non-existing things as 'false', we'll call this the *false-thoughts objection*.

We needn't spend much time on Anselm's answer to the unthinkability objection, because by now it's very familiar: we go about forming a thought of God, painting a mental portrait of God, in the ways we saw in Chapter 2. Though the being we come to think in this way is certainly far removed from the objects of our everyday experience, there is a clear path from those objects to the being than which a greater cannot be thought. We experience good things, and better things, and on that basis we can conceive a being of unsurpassable goodness, one that does not derive its goodness from anything else but is the source of its own goodness and of the goodness of all other good things—and so on for all the other characterizations of the perfect, unlimited, simple God that we derive ultimately from our experience of imperfect, limited, and fragmented creatures.

The false-thoughts objection receives much more of Anselm's attention. He sees that he must show Gaunilo that there are features of our thought of God that guarantee God's existence: as he puts it, 'I say with certainty that if it can be so much as thought to exist, it must necessarily exist'. Anselm offers nine different arguments for the claim that if God can be thought, he must exist in reality, each following the same basic pattern. It is easiest to explain the form of the arguments if we introduce a technical term from contemporary philosophy: merely possible. Something is merely possible if it is (a) possible but (b) non-existent. My older brother Jason is merely possible: (a) my parents could have started their family earlier, and they could have had a boy and named him Jason; but (b) they did not, and in fact I am their firstborn. Anselm's technique is to argue that there are features of our portrait of God that cannot belong to a merely possible being. So, since God is possible—remember, we can't think impossibilities, and we can think God—it follows that God actually exists.

To see how this pattern of argument is supposed to work, let's look at two of the nine versions Anselm offers. In the first version, the feature that cannot belong to a merely possible being is *beginninglessness*:

> That than which a greater cannot be thought cannot be thought of
> as beginning to exist. By contrast, whatever can be thought to exist,
> but does not in fact exist, can be thought of as beginning to exist.

44

Therefore, it is not the case that that than which a greater cannot be thought can be thought to exist, but does not in fact exist. If, therefore, it can be thought to exist, it does necessarily exist.

This is a hard argument to evaluate. Does Anselm mean that any merely possible being can be thought to have a beginning *at some point*, or that any merely possible being can be thought to have a beginning *now*? Consider my merely possible older brother Jason. If he had come to exist, he would have had a beginning in the ordinary way; but it's too late now. If Anselm is arguing that it's too late now for a merely possible beginningless being to exist (because obviously it would have to begin to exist, since it doesn't exist already), that's correct, but hardly relevant. Jason is still a possible being even though it's too late for him to (begin to) exist. So for Anselm's argument to work, he has to mean that any merely possible being can be thought to have a beginning at some point. But is that really the case? It seems to me that I can imagine a merely possible beginningless being: a being that, if it had existed, would never have begun to exist but would have just always been there. Perhaps I am wrong in so thinking, but I can at least see why Gaunilo need not concede yet.

Far more convincing is another feature of that than which a greater cannot be thought that Anselm says cannot belong to a merely possible being: necessary existence. It is obvious that a being that can fail to exist is less great than a being that cannot fail to exist: it has a more tenuous hold on being, it does not have the source of its own being in itself, it must depend on something else to bring it into existence, and so forth. So that than which a greater cannot be thought is a necessary being; it cannot fail to exist. Anselm invites us to get that being before our minds. Does such a being exist in reality? It must. We cannot coherently say 'A being than which a greater cannot be thought is possible but does not exist', because one thing we know about a being than which a greater cannot be thought is that, if it exists, it cannot fail to exist. That is, whatever being we're thinking when we say 'A being than which a greater cannot be thought is possible but does not exist' is not in fact a being than which a greater cannot be thought.

Anselm puts the argument like this:

> Let us assume that [that than which a greater cannot be thought] does not exist, although it can be thought. Now something that can be thought but does not exist would not, if it existed, be that than which a greater cannot be thought. And so, if it existed, that than which a greater cannot be thought would not be that than which a greater cannot be thought, which is utterly absurd. Therefore, if that than which a greater cannot be thought can be thought at all, it is false that it does not exist.

This last claim—if it can be thought, it exists—is the claim that Anselm defends in nine different ways in his reply to Gaunilo. Combined with his argument that it can be thought, this claim gives Anselm a simple, straightforward argument: two premises, both of which he defends, and a conclusion that clearly follows from them. The argument is this:

(1) If that than which a greater cannot be thought can be thought, it exists.

(2) That than which a greater cannot be thought can be thought.

Therefore, (3) that than which a greater cannot be thought exists.

Reformulated in more contemporary language, we have this:

(1) If a perfect being is possible, it exists.
(2) A perfect being is possible.
Therefore, (3) a perfect being exists.

This argument is known as the *modal* ontological argument ('modal' meaning that it has to do with possibility and necessity).

By this point the apparently devastating Lost Island argument has receded from view, and it is hard to see how it would even apply against the modal ontological argument—either in Anselm's formulation or in the contemporary one—because it is not at all parallel to that argument. It does not have the same structure; it does not share (or parody) the same premises. So it is not surprising that Anselm barely mentions the Lost Island in his reply to Gaunilo; he certainly never explains why Gaunilo's argument fails but his own succeeds. Gaunilo thought Anselm's argument relied crucially on the premise that something is greater if it exists in reality than in the understanding alone, but Anselm says he never relied on any such premise. (In fairness to Gaunilo and to generations of interpreters who have followed him, if Anselm did not mean to rely on that premise, his expression in *Proslogion* 2 is clumsy at best.) Instead, Anselm says, that than which a greater cannot be thought has features that cannot belong to a merely possible being. If it is possible—if it can be thought—it must exist.

How God's non-existence is strictly inconceivable

My reading of Anselm's intent in chapter 2 of the *Proslogion* is confirmed by the way he extends the argument in chapter 3. (Some interpreters in fact argue that the 'single argument' extends over chapters 2 and 3.) There he offers a modal argument very much like the one we have already examined from the Reply to Gaunilo. Anselm argues that it is possible to think that something exists that cannot be thought not to exist—something whose non-existence is strictly inconceivable—and that such a being is greater than one that can be thought not to exist. He continues:

> Therefore, if that than which a greater cannot be thought can be
> thought not to exist, then that than which a greater cannot be

thought is *not* that than which a greater cannot be thought; and this is a contradiction. So that than which a greater cannot be thought exists so truly that it cannot even be thought not to exist.

And only when he has established not just the fact of God's existence, but the inconceivability of God's non-existence, does he unequivocally identify that than which a greater cannot be thought with the addressee of his prayer:

And this is you, O Lord our God. You exist so truly, O Lord my God, that you cannot even be thought not to exist. And rightly so, for if some mind could think something better than you, a creature would rise up against the Creator and sit in judgement upon him, which is completely absurd.

Yet it seems this absurdity happens, that people do after all think what Anselm says cannot be thought, namely, that God doesn't exist. For 'the fool has said in his heart, "There is no God"'.

Anselm argues that we must distinguish two senses of 'think' or 'say in one's heart' (he takes those two expressions to be equivalent). In one sense, we think something just by thinking the word that signifies it; in another sense, we think something by understanding what the thing is. Ignorant of physics as I am, I can think quasars and colliders and black holes and string theory in that first sense; but if you press me to explain what I mean, or to evaluate the truth of statements in which those words appear, you will find that I am almost immediately at sea. Those words for me are not even attached to concepts; they are puffs of sound vaguely associated with a particular scientific enterprise, but that's about it. You could even get me to parrot perfectly nonsensical claims—say, 'Quasars are jagged'—and I would have no way of seeing that they're nonsensical. (If spacetime can be curved, whatever that's supposed to mean, quasars might as well be jagged. The one statement conveys no more to me than the other.)

Anselm says that it is in this sense that the Psalmist's fool says in his heart, 'There is no God'. The fool knows the word—he can make the noise or write the letters—but there's no adequate thought *of God* attached to it. If one is really thinking not just the word 'God' but the actual being, one sees that that being must exist: that than which a greater cannot be thought cannot fail to exist.

Is the single argument really a single argument?

By now it should be very clear that Anselm's 'single argument' in the *Proslogion* presupposes a good deal of preliminary intellectual work. Granted, it does not require the 'chaining together of many arguments' that dissatisfied Anselm after he had completed the *Monologion*; but it is also not so simple a matter as entertaining a verbal formula, 'that than which a greater cannot be thought', and doing logical moves with it. Entertaining a verbal formula is the first kind of 'thinking' or 'saying in one's heart', and we have seen that it is wholly inadequate—by Anselm's own account—to establish the existence of the God of Christian belief. One must think God in the second sense: one must get that than which a greater cannot be thought before one's mind, have a thought of it that does not misfire, so that one can see in the contents of that thought the guarantees that the being one is conceiving 'exists as we believe [he] exist[s], and that [he is] what we believe [him] to be'. One must think carefully through what something would have to be in order to be correctly described as 'that than which a greater cannot be thought'—one must paint a pretty detailed portrait of that being—before the single argument from portrait to existing original can work.

Does this mean, then, that Anselm has failed in his effort to provide a 'single argument'? I don't think it does. True, *Proslogion* 2 (or 2 and 3) by itself does not stand alone as an argument for the existence of God. It isn't meant to. But once we have done the preliminary work involved in thinking (in the fullest sense) a being than which a greater cannot be thought, the pattern of reasoning provided in *Proslogion* 2 and 3 is all we need to establish the existence of such a being. It also gives us everything we need to derive all the standard divine attributes, as we see throughout the rest of the *Proslogion*: for example,

> Then what are you, Lord God, than which nothing greater can be thought? What are you, if not the greatest of all beings, who alone exists through himself and made all other things from nothing? For whatever is not this is less than the greatest that can be thought, but this cannot be thought of you. What good is missing from the supreme good, through which every good thing exists? And so you are just, truthful, happy, and whatever it is better to be than not to be. For it is better to be just than unjust, and better to be happy than unhappy.

And there is at least one further way in which the *Proslogion* argument represents an advance on, and a radical simplification of, the complicated series of arguments in the *Monologion*. In the *Monologion* the various divine attributes for which Anselm argues piecemeal are, to all appearances, an assortment of features, not unified in any obvious way, for all that some of them appear to entail others. What makes it on the list seems to be determined more by Scripture and tradition than by the demands of reason. But in the *Proslogion* we have a unifying concept and a unifying pattern of argument that explain why those features are on the list: because they, and only they, are the features that belong to a being than which a greater cannot be thought.

Chapter 4
How things got started

The conception of a being than which a greater cannot be thought is a powerful one: it generates an impressive list of divine attributes, unifies them conceptually, and even reveals that such a being cannot fail to exist. But it doesn't tell us everything there is to know about God. Readers familiar with standard Christian doctrine may have noticed two sizeable omissions thus far: the doctrine that God is the Creator and the doctrine of the Trinity. Anselm does not try to argue that it is greater to be a creator than not to be a creator, nor does he try to argue that it is greater to be a Trinity than not to be a Trinity.

God the Creator

There was at least some room in the tradition for an argument that it is greater to be a creator than not. One strand of Platonism taught that goodness tends to diffuse or share itself (*bonum diffusivum sui*). On that view it would be natural for an unsurpassably great being to communicate its goodness to other things: being a creator, or at least a source of other good things, would be an essential characteristic of a wholly good being. Anselm does not explicitly address that way of thinking, but it's clear enough why it wouldn't appeal to him. That than which a greater cannot be thought is wholly and unsurpassably good in himself, utterly self-sufficient, needing nothing outside himself in order to express or exemplify his goodness. A God who can't be God without creating is no God at all.

And suppose for a moment—just for the sake of argument—that it *is* necessary for a perfectly good being to 'diffuse' his goodness to other things. Is this diffusion a result of that being's choice, or does it just happen? Neither answer is tenable. If it just happens, creatures flow forth from God (the traditional expression is 'emanate') independently of God's own intention, which undermines divine ultimacy and omnipotence. If God must choose to create, there's something outside of God that constrains or compels his choice, which undermines divine aseity. So Anselm's view is that God is equally great—equally God—whether he creates or not. We know he is a Creator because we know that things other than God exist, and given divine ultimacy and aseity, that means that God brought them into being by a free and uncompelled choice.

Anselm explores the doctrine of creation at some length in the *Monologion*, an exploration that leads somewhat surprisingly to the other missing doctrine, the Trinity. When he first raises the relationship of other things to God in chapter 7 of the *Monologion*, all he has established up to that point is that all things other than God exist through God and from God. So Anselm asks what this means: in what way do all other things exist through and from God? It is not that some of God's matter provided the 'stuff' of which other things were made: 'if something less than the supreme nature can exist from the matter of the supreme nature, the supreme good can be changed and corrupted—which it is impious to say'. Nor is it that God merely helped something else make them, or formed pre-existing matter into things. Instead, all things other than God—including matter itself—are from God in the sense that he made them, as their chief and principal cause, unassisted by any other.

Anselm was fascinated by the language of causation throughout his career, returning to different fine-grained analyses of causal language again and again in his treatises. (He also left some unfinished writings on the subject in what we call the Lambeth Fragments.) Since he is open to using the word *facere*, to make or bring about, in so many different ways, it is important here to note that he understands God's making or bringing about creatures as causality in the most basic and direct sense. God acts knowingly and intentionally, and everything other than God is an effect of that intentional act.

We have an intuitive feel for this sort of bringing-about, because we experience causation all the time. I move my fingers in a certain way over the keyboard and thereby cause a bit of Bach to be played. I may not be able to say much about the mechanics—how the keys, the hammers, and the strings all work together in producing the sound—but I have no doubt that I have just brought about some music. I have experienced causation, and I myself was the cause. This sort of causation, which philosophers call 'efficient causation', is the kind of causality Anselm is ascribing to God with respect to creation.

Yet although we can say that God's causality is of the same *kind* as the causality we experience in our own actions and in the world around us, God's exercise of that kind of causality is quite different from ours. I need a piano to play, air for singing, paper on which to write and a pen to discharge the ink, my natural powers of mind to generate thoughts and arrange them. That is, I exercise my efficient-causal powers on things that already exist, using powers that ultimately belong to my nature: and my nature is not something that I have from myself.

God, by contrast, has (or rather is) his nature *a se*, from himself, and he does not require pre-existing things on which to exercise his causal power. Moreover, God's causality cannot be impeded, as ours can: both my natural powers and the objects on which I exercise them can fail me to various degrees. I want to sing, but my laryngitis is atrocious; I want to jot down a note, but the paper is wet and, anyway, my hand is shaking. God simply wills, and it is so.

The Word

God's act of creation is, therefore, an efficacious act; but it is also an intentional act. It is in exploring the intentionality of God's creative act that Anselm begins to introduce the doctrine of the Trinity. There is, Anselm says, 'no way anyone could make something rationally unless something like a pattern (or, to put it more suitably, a form or likeness or rule) of the thing to be made already existed in the reason of the maker'. And of course God's causality is not the automatic causality of one billiard ball hitting another; what God does, he means to do. So we can conclude that 'what creatures were going to be, and what sorts of things, and how they were going to be, was in the reason of the supreme nature before all things were made'. The creatures themselves did not exist, for God made everything from nothing; and yet they were not entirely nothing, because their patterns or images were something in the divine mind.

Consider a craftsman. Before he makes his work, he conceives it; then he executes the work in accordance with his conception. That conception, Anselm says, is a kind of mental utterance: the craftsman 'says his work within himself by a conception of his mind'. There are various kinds of mental utterance, but the most exact and expressive mental utterance is 'the likeness that is expressed in the gaze of the mind of someone who is thinking the thing itself'. This is the kind of conception God has of the things he is going to make.

The comparison falls short in a number of ways, some obvious and some not so obvious. One obvious way is that even the most imaginative human craftsman collects the materials for his mental conception from other things he has experienced—even if he then does something quite startling and unexpected with those materials as he forms them into a mental utterance—and then executes that conception using pre-existing stuff that he shapes and arranges according to his conception. Neither of these limitations applies to the Craftsman who is the sole, total, and complete cause of everything that is not himself.

Less obviously, the human craftsman's conception is not identical with the craftsman himself, or even with the craftsman's mind. My thought of the Bach prelude I have memorized and am about to play is not me; it is not my mind; it is just one among many thoughts that I can assemble, entertain, recall, and even forget. God has no such accidents and is not subject to change. Most important for Anselm, however, is the fact that God cannot depend on anything other than himself to be or to do what he is or does. So God's utterance of creation is God himself. As Anselm puts it,

> Now since by the teaching of reason it is equally certain that, whatever the supreme substance made, he did not make it through anything other than himself, and that whatever he made, he made it through his innermost utterance (whether by saying individual things by means of individual words, or instead by saying all things at once by means of one word), what could be any more necessary than this: the utterance of the supreme essence is nothing other than the supreme essence?

Anselm's switch from the language of utterance (*locutio*) to that of word (*verbum*) in this passage is not a mere stylistic variant. The Scriptural images of the creative act as divine speech—'And God said, "Let light be made", and light was made'; 'He spoke and it came to pass, he commanded and they were created'; 'By the word of the Lord were the heavens made'—have their decisive theological interpretation for Christians in the Prologue to the Gospel according to John: 'In the beginning was the Word, and the Word was with God, and the Word was God. He was in the beginning with God. All things were made through him, and without him was not anything made that was made'. This dense passage makes at least four theological claims that Anselm is concerned to defend and elucidate as part of his project of faith seeking understanding. I take them in the logical order of Anselm's exposition, rather than in their textual order in John.

First, 'In the beginning was the Word'. That is, before there was any creation—before there was even any 'before'—God had a plan, a blueprint, for the creation that he was going to make, as all rational agents have an idea of any intentional act before they perform it. This blueprint is best thought of as an internal utterance or word. Second, 'all things were made through the Word, and without the Word was not anything made that was made'. God's internal utterance of the creation that he intentionally brings about is complete: there is no created thing for which there was not a blueprint. Third, 'the Word was God'. As we have already seen, Anselm argues that whatever God makes, he makes through God; so if God makes creation through the Word, the Word is God.

Now at this point we could suppose that 'the Word was God' is just another expression of divine simplicity: just as divine power = God, and divine justice = God, and divine eternity = God, so too the divine utterance of creation = God. But how then will we understand the fourth and most difficult claim: 'the Word was with God'? One thing can only be *with* another thing. How are God and the Word two, rather than simply one? And two *whats*?

Anselm has two arguments for the claim that the Word is not altogether the same thing as the supreme spirit ('the Word was with God'), even though the Word *is* the supreme spirit ('the Word was God'). First, if something is true of x that is not true of y, x and y are not altogether the same thing. Now the supreme spirit is an utterer and not a Word, whereas the Word is a Word and not an utterer. So the supreme spirit and the Word are not altogether the same thing. Second, the supreme spirit and the Word bear relations to each other that one thing cannot bear to itself. Philosophers call these 'irreflexive relations', though Anselm does not have that terminology. Examples of irreflexive relations include *being older than* and *being greater than*: a thing cannot be older than itself or greater than itself. In the case of the supreme spirit and the Word, we have at least two irreflexive relations by which they are distinguished: *being the Word of* and *existing from*. The Word is the Word of the supreme spirit, and nothing can be the Word of itself; the Word exists from the supreme spirit, and nothing can exist from itself. Therefore, the supreme spirit and the Word are not altogether one; they are in some respect two.

But again we ask: two *whats*? There really is no appropriate noun, Anselm says. They are not two gods, or two supreme spirits, or two almighties, or two creators: there is one divine nature, and we can speak only in the singular of the divine nature or anything that characterizes the divine nature. After forty-something chapters of avoiding a noun altogether, Anselm finally settles on 'person' or 'substance'—'person' was the traditional word in Western theology, 'substance' in Eastern theology—'for lack of a strictly appropriate word'. (For the designation of the supreme spirit and the Word as 'Father' and 'Son', see the box entitled 'Why "Father"?'.)

The simple Word and the complexity of creation

When Anselm first introduced the divine utterance of creation, he left it open whether God would utter creation by means of a single word or many words: 'whatever he made, he made it through his innermost utterance (whether by saying individual things by means of individual words, or instead by saying all things at once by means of one word)'. Now that he has identified that utterance with the Word who is with God, and is God, Anselm can resolve that issue: the Word is God, and God is supremely simple, so the Word is supremely simple. The Word by which God utters creation is one Word.

Why 'Father'?

In the *Monologion* Anselm does not use the word 'God' (*Deus*) until the final chapter. Up to that point he refers to 'the supreme essence', 'the supreme nature', and 'the supreme spirit'. The words for 'essence' and 'nature' are feminine, and 'spirit' is masculine (as 'God' also is); 'Word' is neuter. Why, then, the exclusively masculine language of 'Father' and 'Son'? It is a mark of Anselm's independence of mind, and of the thoroughness of his project of faith seeking understanding, that he sees the need to raise this question. There is no distinction of sex in them, Anselm says (the point is so obvious it doesn't even require argument), so why not 'Mother' and 'Daughter' just as appropriately as 'Father' and 'Son'? You can't say it's because they are both spirit (which is grammatically masculine), since they are also both truth and wisdom (which are grammatically feminine). You can't say it's because in sexually dimorphic animals the male is always stronger and better than the female, because that's not even true. Instead, the reason is that 'the first and principal cause of offspring is always in the father'. The mother is a secondary cause. It would be inappropriate to apply a word designating a secondary or inferior cause to 'that parent who begets his offspring without any other cause that either accompanies or precedes him'. So the divine parent is a father: and since a son is always more like a father than a daughter is, we should call the divine offspring, who is the perfect image of the Father, a son.

Anselm thus has no argument for 'Father' and 'Son' apart from his mistaken biology. Whether he would be sympathetic to the contemporary impulse to avoid masculine language for God, or instead seek some other argument to uphold the traditional language, is something we cannot know. It is worth noting, however, that long before Julian of Norwich famously addressed Jesus as 'Mother' in her *Revelations of Divine Love*, Anselm

addressed not only Jesus but also Paul as 'Mother' at great length
in his 'Prayer to Saint Paul', from which a brief excerpt follows:

Therefore, you are both mothers.

Yes, you are fathers, but you are nonetheless also mothers.

For you have brought it about—

you, Jesus, through yourself; you, Paul, through him—

that we who are born into death are reborn into life.

So you are fathers in the power of your effect,

mothers in the tenderness of your affection;

fathers in authority,

mothers in gentleness;

fathers in protecting us,

mothers in pitying us.

Therefore, you are both mothers.

How, then, do we account for the variety and differentiation
among created things? Augustine, drawing on the same craftsman
analogy that Anselm uses, had argued that of course God must
have different conceptions (*rationes*) for different creatures; it
would be absurd to think that God makes a human being and
a horse by the same conception. There is a divine idea of a horse,
a divine idea of a human being, and so on for each kind of
creature; these ideas are in the Word. The apparatus of divine
ideas served both a metaphysical and an epistemological function.
Metaphysically, it offered an account of universals—that is, of
what all things of the same kind have in common—that satisfied
both the Platonic intuition that universals are real and the
Christian requirement that nothing, not even universals, exists

independently of God. Epistemologically, it explained how there can be general or universal knowledge: knowledge, not of this horse and that horse, but of *what it is to be a horse*.

Anselm's insistence on the unity of the Word deprives him of these resources. There is no question that Anselm thinks universals are real, and that we have universal and not merely particular knowledge, but he does not construct a systematic account of universals or even give us the materials with which we might construct such an account on his behalf. Where Augustine would say that the Word *contains* the blueprint for all creatures, Anselm says that the Word *is* the blueprint for all creatures. Yet creatures—limited, changing, and fragmented as they are—are wildly unlike the infinite, immutable, and simple Word. How, then, do we make sense of the claim that the Word is the blueprint of creation? Anselm sees the difficulty clearly: 'If the Word has no likeness to mutable things, how is it that they were patterned after him?'

Anselm asks us to consider the relation between a human being and a painting of a human being. The reality of humanity is in an actual human being; in the painting there is a likeness or image of that reality. Similarly, the reality of existence is in the Word; in creatures there is a likeness or image of that reality. You could even say, in one sense, that the Word alone exists (just as you can say that nothing is human except a living human being) because the Word alone, as divine, possesses perfect and unlimited existence. In another sense, however, creatures exist as well, because they have been made by the Word and in accordance with the Word. As the painting is an imitation of the living original, creatures are an imitation of the Word. The greater their resemblance to the Word, the greater their being: living creatures are greater than non-living, creatures capable of perception are greater still, and rational creatures are the greatest of all, because they imitate the Word as closely as any creature can. But the Word in no way depends on creatures to exist, or even to be a Word, any more than a human being depends on his portrait to exist or to be a human being. The Word is the Word of God, not (as it turns out) the Word of creation, because the Word is a perfect likeness of God and not at all a likeness of creation, though creation is a likeness of the Word.

This is, to be sure, a difficult position to make sense of. Part of the difficulty is that we think of the relation of *being like* as what we nowadays call a symmetric relation. In a symmetric relation, if x bears that relation to y, y also bears it to x. *Being like* seems like a strong candidate for being a symmetric relation: if I am like my sister, my sister is like me. So if creatures are like the Word, surely the Word is like creatures. But for Anselm the relevant relation is not *being like*, but *being a likeness of*, which is quite plausibly taken as an asymmetric relation. We might say that if my portrait is like me, I am like my portrait; but we would certainly not say that if my portrait is a likeness of me, I am a likeness of my portrait. It is in precisely this sense that creatures are a likeness of the Word but the Word is not a likeness of creatures.

This explanation gets us some way towards understanding Anselm's view of the relationship between creation and the Word, but the notion of likeness (or resemblance or imitation—he uses all these expressions) leaves some mysteries unresolved. One such mystery is how different creatures imitate the Word in different ways. Anselm offers us a way of understanding how a human being imitates the Word both in a different way and in a more excellent way than a cat does: the human being has reason, whereas the cat has only the power of sensation. But how does a dog imitate the Word in a different way from a cat? It's hard to see an answer, and yet presumably creatures can be different from one another only insofar as they imitate the Word in different ways.

Truth

Whatever the solution to this problem (if Anselm even sees it as a problem) might be, Anselm does provide a basis for the differentiation of creatures, not in a version of the doctrine of divine ideas, but instead in his notion of truth. I spoke earlier of the *reality* of human being, which exists in a living human being, as opposed to the image of that reality existing in a painting. The word Anselm uses for 'reality' in that passage is *veritas*, 'truth', and Anselm devotes a short dialogue, *On Truth* (see Figure 2), to a wide-ranging exploration of the concept of truth, which in turn informs his accounts of free choice and of the fall, to which we will turn in the next chapter.

Ordinarily when we think of truth, we think of the truth of statements. If I say 'It is day' when in fact it is day, my statement is true; if I say 'It is day' when in fact it is night, my statement is false. There may be great philosophical complexities lurking underneath this apparently simple characterization of truth—the notion of truth is endlessly disputed by philosophers—but Anselm is happy to start with the common-sense account that any of his readers will be able to understand. Instead of asking whether this is an adequate account of truth, he accepts the account, as far as it goes, and poses a further question: *why* do we call a statement true when it successfully states the way things are? The reason, he says, is that this is what statements *ought to do*: 'when a statement signifies that what-is is, it signifies what it ought to' and so 'its signification is correct'. The truth of a statement is its correctness (*rectitudo*), and correctness is a matter of something's being or doing what it ought to be or do. Once we think of truth in that way, we can see that the concept is applicable in many domains, beyond that of language.

Some of these domains are more intuitively obvious than others. There is truth in opinions, clearly, because rational creatures

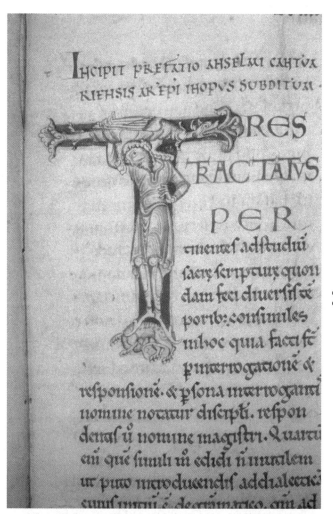

2. An illuminated capital begins the preface to an early manuscript of Anselm's dialogues *On Truth*, *On Freedom of Choice*, and *On the Fall of the Devil*.

received their intellectual capacity in order to represent to themselves the way things really are. When we think that what-is is, or that what-is-not is not, we are thinking what we ought to think, and so our thought or opinion is correct and true. Less obviously, there is truth in an action when something does what it ought to do, truth in the senses when they report sense objects in the way they ought to report them, and truth in what Anselm calls 'the being of things' when things are as they ought to be.

Although Anselm does not explicitly put his account of truth to this use, it provides a clear basis for the differentiation of creatures, not in terms of the different ways in which they imitate the Word, but instead in terms of the different natures, causal powers, and purposes that God has bestowed on them. For example, in speaking of truth in action, Anselm says that 'fire received the power to heat from the one from whom it has being', which is why we can say that when fire heats, it is doing what it ought to do, or 'doing the truth'. There is truth in our senses when they perceive a straight stick partly submerged in water as bent, because they are doing what God gave them the power to do. The human flesh that was pierced by nails and suffered terrible pain on the Cross ought to have been pierced, and ought to have suffered, because God created flesh that way. The existence, capacities, powers, and purposes of every creature are bestowed by God, and so just as creation in general is an effect of God's intentional action, the variety and differentiation among creatures is an effect of God's intentional action.

Most creatures cannot fail to 'do the truth': they have no choice in the matter. Fire heats, celestial bodies move, horses graze, plants grow, all according to their natures, and they cannot deviate from truth or correctness. Anselm calls the actions of such creatures 'natural actions', because they flow straightforwardly from the natures God bestowed on them. But God gave some creatures a capacity for self-determination—the will (*voluntas*)—that is not simply the working-out of a nature. Such 'non-natural' or voluntary actions can deviate from truth and correctness. There is truth in our wills when we will what we ought to will, in accordance with the purpose for which God gave us wills. In the next chapter I look in detail at Anselm's account of the will, God's purpose in creating it, and how both angels and human beings abandoned truth in the will.

Chapter 5
How things went wrong

There are three courses of events, Anselm says: miraculous, natural, and voluntary. Miraculous events come about by God's will alone. The initial act of creation counts as a miraculous act: 'it was God's will alone that made the natures of things in the beginning'. Having made those natures, God remains free to use them to accomplish what they would never do of themselves. These further miraculous acts—the parting of the Red Sea, the raising of the dead, the turning of water into wine—do not 'do creatures any injury when they appear to supersede creatures, since creatures have nothing but what they received from God'.

Apart from miracles, then, created beings act in accordance with the natures God gave them. They 'do the truth', exercising the powers they received from God. But Anselm holds that in addition to the miraculous and the natural, there is a third category: the voluntary. Voluntary actions proceed neither from God's will nor from a creature's nature, but from a creature's will (*voluntas*).

Justice

Now what exactly a will is, and why Anselm thinks we have to recognize this third category—actions that proceed neither from God's will nor from a creature's nature, but from a creature's will—requires a good bit of conceptual excavation. In his dialogue

On Truth, having reached the definition of truth as correctness that is perceptible only by the mind, the student who is Anselm's interlocutor proposes that such correctness seems to be the same thing as justice: if it is right or correct for something to be the way it is, then it is just for it to be the way it is, and vice versa. Yet this seems odd: it is right or correct for the stone to fall to the ground when I let go of it, but surely we wouldn't say that the stone, or its fall, is just.

No, we don't usually say that, Anselm replies (though—he seems to imply—we could). What the student is looking for is 'a definition of the justice that deserves praise, just as its opposite, injustice, deserves reproach'. We don't praise the stone for falling to the ground. We don't praise a horse for grazing. We do, however, praise (or blame) rational creatures for at least some of their actions.

Anselm takes it as uncontroversial that our ascriptions of justice and injustice are well-grounded—not that we're infallible in making those ascriptions, of course, but that there genuinely is something about actions in virtue of which they can rightly be praised or blamed. The question is how justice and injustice are possible. What must be true of us, what powers must we have, what conditions must God have set up, in order for us to be the sorts of beings who are capable of acting justly or unjustly? Or, to put the same question in another way, what do we have that stones and horses don't have?

One obvious thing is that we have reason. Unlike a stone or a horse, a rational being can know what it ought to do. We don't call stones or horses just, because they do what is correct unknowingly. (This is not to say that, for example, horses don't know that they're grazing, that the grass is delicious, or what have you; but they can't have thoughts along the lines of 'Grazing is the right thing for me as a horse to do'.) Only a being that can know what is correct—a being that is 'aware of rectitude', as Anselm puts it—can be praiseworthy for anything. But being aware of rectitude is not enough for justice; one can know what is right and refuse to act accordingly. Even willing—wanting or choosing—what one knows is right might not be enough, because one might will it for the wrong reason. I know that I ought to give generously to the poor, but I don't actually care about the poor; I care about the reputation I will gain when other people see my generous act, which I will of course take care to publicize. I am willing what I know I ought to will, so I have not only awareness of rectitude but even rectitude of will, but I am not just.

As Anselm puts it, 'Every will has a what and a why'. In the situation I've described, the what is correct but the why is not. Justice requires that both be correct. Anselm accordingly defines justice as 'correctness (*rectitudo*) of will preserved for its own sake'. First, justice is correctness *of will*: it is wanting what one ought to want. Second, it is preserved *for its own sake*, that is, for the sake of justice itself, not because one is seeking a reward or avoiding a punishment or acting under compulsion. Third, it is *preserved* because the initial possession of an upright will is a gift of God: I cannot cause myself to have an upright will any more than I can cause myself to exist in the first place. I do, however, have the power to preserve that uprightness of will, and to preserve it for the sake of uprightness itself. It is because rational beings have this power that they can rightly be called just or unjust.

Free choice

The power to preserve uprightness of will for its own sake—in other words, the power for justice—is what Anselm calls 'free choice' or 'freedom of choice'. (He uses those expressions interchangeably.) Free choice, in other words, is defined explicitly in terms of its moral purpose: it is a power for justice. Both in Anselm's day and our own, discussions of freedom often assume that freedom is something like the ability to choose among genuinely open alternatives. Anselm entertains such an understanding of freedom at the very beginning of his dialogue *On Freedom of Choice*, only to dismiss it immediately.

Anselm's student-interlocutor opens the dialogue by asking why we ever need grace if 'freedom of choice is "the ability to sin and not to sin", as some are accustomed to say, and we always have that ability'. Anselm replies that the ability to sin cannot be part of the definition of free choice, because God and the good angels are free, but they cannot sin. The student does not question what Anselm says about God and the good angels and their freedom, but the background assumptions that allow the student and teacher to agree so quickly are worth stating explicitly. We know already that God is just and cannot sin: Anselm establishes that explicitly in the *Proslogion*. That there are good angels who cannot sin was a well-entrenched view in the Christian theological tradition. The good angels are praiseworthy, and therefore just. Since free choice is simply the power for justice, then, both God and the good angels, being just, must also be free.

In fact, Anselm argues, they are freer than human beings are. Freedom is essentially purposive: it is the power to preserve rectitude of will for its own sake, the power to maintain justice. God and the good angels are just in such a way that they cannot lose justice: God because he *is* his own justice and cannot cease to be himself, the good angels for reasons that we will find out about in due course. Human beings are just (if they are just at all) in such a way that they can lose justice. Clearly, 'someone who has what is fitting and expedient in such a way that he cannot lose it is freer than someone who has it in such a way that he can lose it and be seduced into what is unfitting and inexpedient'.

The word 'seduced' is carefully chosen. Anselm argues that nothing can compel a just human being to abandon rectitude of will. However attractive a temptation is, an upright will has the power to cling to rectitude of will, to preserve that rectitude for the sake of rectitude itself. That power is precisely what free choice is. Yet clearly we do not always exercise that power according to its intended purpose; we do not always uphold justice or 'do the truth'. If free choice is not the power to sin or not to sin, how is it that, when we do sin, we sin freely? Or perhaps more pointedly, why does God create human beings who are capable of sinning if the power to sin is not needed in order for a being to be just and praiseworthy?

Anselm's fullest and most compelling answers to these questions are found in his dialogue *On the Fall of the Devil*. There, instead of beginning with the concept of free choice and working outward to its implications, as he does in *On Freedom of Choice*, he starts with what he takes to be the facts on the ground, so to speak, and asks what has to be true in order to make sense of those facts.

'What do you have that you did not receive?'

The dialogue opens with what to modern sensibilities is an undeniably strange question from the student-interlocutor: 'When the Apostle [Paul] says "What do you have that you did not receive?", is he saying this only to human beings, or to angels as well?' The idea that St Paul would have angels in mind as part of the audience for his First Letter to the Corinthians is so alien to the historical-critical reading of Scripture we take for granted nowadays that it might be hard for us even to take the student's question seriously. It also raises echoes of the complaint that medieval theologians were bizarrely obsessed with angels, as in the much-mocked query 'How many angels can dance on the head of a pin?'

In fact there is no record of any medieval thinker asking that question; it is an early-modern jibe made by people who did not understand the function that angels served in medieval theology. Angels served a purpose much like that of the often quite outlandish thought experiments used in contemporary philosophy: they allowed thinkers to isolate the essential features of the topic they were investigating. Focusing on angels allows Anselm to set aside some of the complications peculiar to the human situation so that he can get clear on the essentials of freedom, choice, and sin. Human beings face many choices, some of them between right and wrong, but others arguably of no moral significance. (Except under some contrived circumstances that a philosopher might invent, it surely makes no moral difference whether I dip my French fries in mayonnaise or in ketchup.) We come to these choices already shaped by heredity, experience, education, and temperament. We encounter temptations; we suffer from ignorance. We are also afflicted, Anselm holds, with the inherited injustice that is original sin, and we need grace to overcome it.

The case of the fall of the angels avoids all these complexities. According to tradition, the angels faced a single choice, and it was of paramount moral significance: whether to submit to God or rebel against God. They had suffered no damage to their nature; they were in the original state in which God had created them. So the case of the angels provides a perfect case for examining how choice itself, as opposed to choice under highly peculiar conditions, actually works. Angels are a bit like frictionless surfaces in physics: a theoretically fruitful idealization—except that angels, unlike frictionless surfaces, actually exist (or at least so the medievals thought).

Paul's question to the Corinthians also highlights what for Anselm is the central problem that his account of the fall has to solve. When Paul asks, 'What do you have that you did not receive?', he expects the answer 'Nothing', as is evident from the question that immediately follows: 'Why then do you boast as if you had not received?' The Corinthians had been boasting of their spiritual gifts, forgetting that gifts are just that: gifts received from God, not personal accomplishments to boast about. But if it really is true that everything we have is received from God—our reason, our wills, our desires, our choices—then in what way is anything at all up to us? If we have something good, we received it from God, and so have nothing to boast about; and if we lack something good, we lack it only because God didn't give it to us, and so we have nothing to be blamed for.

Concerning the fall of the angels, Augustine had argued that God gave all angels a just will, but he did not give all angels perseverance in that just will. The angels who were given perseverance stood firm in obedience to God; the angels who were not given perseverance rebelled, falling into the privation of good into which all things created from nothing tend to fall. Anselm, however, sees very clearly that this account makes God, not the angels themselves, responsible for the fall of the angels. If the angels have nothing that they did not receive from God, then the difference between the good angels and the fallen angels derives, not from the angels themselves, but from God. God omits to give perseverance to some of the angels, and they cannot have perseverance if they don't receive it.

Such a conclusion impugns the justice of God: he would be withholding a gift from the angels and then punishing them for lacking it. (Anselm is also no great fan of the Augustinian idea that anything created from nothing has a tendency to relapse into nothingness. He never deals with it explicitly, but judging by his careful analysis in the *Monologion* of what it means for creatures to be created from nothing, and by his insistence that there was not anything either pushing or pulling the will into sin, I would say he thinks Augustine got a bit carried away with a metaphor.) Moreover, if an angel denied the gift of perseverance was unable to persevere, as Augustine's account assumes, such an angel would have lacked the power to preserve rectitude of will for its own sake: in other words, the angel would have lacked free choice and therefore had no power to be just, and consequently would not be subject to either praise or blame.

The primal angelic choice

Anselm seeks an account of the primal angelic choice that upholds both God's justice and the angels' free choice, without running afoul of the idea that everything good creatures have is received from God. His first move in constructing the account is to say that Augustine had the order of explanation backwards. It's not correct to say that the angels who fell did not receive perseverance because God did not give it; rather, God did not give it because they did not receive it. If you offer me a gift and I decline it, my not receiving the gift is the cause of your not giving it, and not the other way around. The angels were all offered the gift of perseverance—the gift of retaining the justice God had given them—but some of them refused it. Instead they abandoned justice, though God had given them the power to retain it. Why did they abandon justice? It must have been because they preferred something else, which they could not have unless they abandoned justice.

There are, at the most general level, only two sorts of things that rational beings can want: justice and what Anselm calls 'advantageous things' (*commoda*). Advantageous things are those that make us happy, or at least those we think will make us happy: pleasure, friendship, a glittering reputation, the gratifying sensation of having escaped a conversation with a tedious colleague by disappearing down a side corridor. The angels could not have abandoned justice for the sake of justice, obviously, so they must have abandoned it for the sake of something advantageous, something 'that they did not have and ought not to have willed at that time, but that could have served to increase their happiness'. Anselm commendably says he does not know what that advantageous thing was—how exactly are we to know what might make an angel happy?—and is content to call it *illud plus*: 'that something more' or 'that additional bit'.

The good angels, Anselm reasons, must have had the same power as the angels who fell to abandon justice for the sake of that something more. Otherwise, 'they would have preserved justice out of necessity and not in virtue of their power'. They would not have been just, because justice is rectitude of will preserved for its own sake, not by nature or under coercion or for the sake of same extraneous reward. Nor would they have been praiseworthy. There has to be an equal playing field among all the angels before their primal choice: they must have the same rational powers, the same freedom, the same information, the same open alternative between retaining justice (and retaining it for its own sake) and abandoning justice for the sake of that something more.

The basic logic here is clear. If the explanation for why some angels remained steadfast (as Anselm likes to put it) and others fell is some difference in the angels' powers or initial circumstances, then God, not the angels themselves, will be responsible for the steadfastness of the good angels and the rebellion of the bad. The good will not deserve their reward, nor the bad their punishment. For it is God and God alone who gave the angels their powers and placed them in the circumstances of the primal choice.

Yet the very lucidity of this reasoning exposes two considerable difficulties for Anselm's account. First, it seems to force Anselm to say that there is something the angels bring about—namely, their primal choice for either justice or advantage—that God does not bring about. But that would surely violate the spirit of the Pauline question with which the dialogue opens, 'What do you have that you did not receive?' Instead of the expected answer, 'Nothing', it seems that all the angels could say, 'Our primal choice of justice over advantage' (or vice versa).

Second, Anselm's reasoning seems to require open alternatives for free choice and, consequently, for justice. The angels must be able to choose between justice and advantage: otherwise, they will be acting out of necessity rather than freely. Yet Anselm has been quite clear that alternative possibilities are not essential for freedom. Is he simply being inconsistent on that point?

The structure of rational choice

Anselm does not pose these two questions to himself, but the way in which the dialogue develops makes it clear that he has considered them and has answers for them. The answers come by way of a series of thought experiments in which Anselm and his student construct the essential scaffolding for the angels' choice. To begin, 'let's suppose that right now God is making an angel that he wills to make happy, and he's not making the angel all at once but rather part by part'. At the hypothetical first stage, the angel is 'apt to have a will' but does not yet will anything. Can the angel, using the powers God has already given him, move himself to will something?

No, Anselm says, because whatever moves itself to will, first wills to move itself. This sounds as if Anselm is setting up an infinite regress—in order to will anything at all, I must move to will myself to move to will myself to move, *ad infinitum*—but really the point is much more straightforward. If there's nothing at all that I want, I don't have the wherewithal to start wanting anything. So before the angel can will anything, God must give him a will. God wants the angel to be happy, and no one can be happy unless he wills happiness, so God gives the angel a will for happiness. But no one deserves to be happy unless he also wills justice, so God also gives the angel a will for justice.

If some of this exposition seems confusing, that's because the Latin *voluntas*, which we translate as 'will', is ambiguous. 'It has three senses', Anselm explains: 'the instrument for willing, the affection of the instrument, and the uses of that instrument'. Will as instrument is the power we exercise when we choose, as vision is the power we exercise when we see and reason is the power we exercise when we think. Latin lacks articles, but in English we can pick out will as instrument by the use of the definite article: *the* will. Will as affection refers to various dispositions of *the* will. It is in this sense of 'will' that I can say I have a will to be healthy even when I am not actively making a choice to be healthy, or even thinking about health one way or the other. Will as use refers to the exercise of *the* will: to choices or volitions. In his psychological construction of the angel, Anselm is arguing that a bare will (will as instrument), without any dispositions (will as affection), cannot move itself to will (will as use). So God shapes the angel's will by giving it two affections, a will for happiness and a will for justice.

But why two affections? If the only role of an affection or disposition is to make an angel capable of willing, it seems that one would do—especially one as broad as the will for happiness. So Anselm invites us to imagine the angel-under-construction being given only the will for happiness. Yes, in virtue of his will for happiness, the angel could move himself to will any number of things for the sake of happiness. But he could will things only for the sake of happiness, and he could not refrain from willing advantageous things: the more advantageous the thing, the stronger his willing. He would will the best advantageous things he knew about, even if it were not fitting for him to will them; he would will the very 'lowest advantageous things, the impure things in which irrational animals take pleasure', if he thought those were the only advantageous things he could have. But in no case would his will be either just or unjust, because he would be willing exactly what God gave him the power to will: happiness, and nothing else. So his will (that's will as use—his volitions) would be 'the work and gift of God'. The angel would be no more praiseworthy or blameworthy for his willing than a stone is for falling to the earth.

Similar considerations apply if the angel is given only the will for justice. Now he can will only what is just and fitting. The angel cannot be unjust, because he can will only justice. But neither can he be just, because he cannot will justice for its own sake; he wills justice by necessity, because that is all he received the power to will. Once again, his will is 'the work and gift of God'.

But if the angel has both wills—both affections—he has the power to make a choice that isn't a necessary outgrowth of the nature and powers God gave him, but instead an act that genuinely belongs to the angel as its initiator or agent. In the situation of the primal choice, all the angels have both the affection for justice and the affection for happiness. They can exercise their will-as-instrument by forgoing advantage ('that something more') for the sake of justice; they can also exercise their will by choosing advantage and thereby abandoning justice. Nothing about what God does—creating them as they are, revealing to them what they know, placing them in the circumstances in which they find themselves—makes the difference between the angels who remain steadfast and the angels who fall. It is the angels themselves who make the difference by freely willing one way or the other.

So it does turn out after all that the angels can answer St Paul's question, 'What do you have that you did not receive?', with 'Our free choice of justice over advantage' (or vice versa) rather than the 'Nothing' that Paul expects. Anselm sees as clearly as anyone before or since, and much more clearly than most, that if the answer really is 'Nothing'—if absolutely everything belonging to a creature, including every choice, is received from God—there will be no real responsibility or agency on the part of any creature. All creaturely choices will be 'the work and gift of God'.

Anselm is here making a radical break with the Augustinian tradition, which insisted that everything that is good, including our own good choices, is from God; we can mar the good we receive, but we cannot bring about any good in ourselves by our own powers. Anselm says otherwise: good choices are things, and the good angels bring about those good things. Still, we can rightly say (by way of placating Paul and Augustine) that God brought about the choice of the good angels, provided that we understand that to mean that God brought about the angels' power of choice and left them free to exercise it. But in a similar way we can rightly say (by way of exasperating Paul and Augustine) that the good angels gave themselves justice, provided that we understand that to mean that the good angels had the power to abandon justice but did not. Our causal language has to be stretched a bit so as to accommodate both the tradition and Anselm's radical modification of that tradition.

The central imperative of finding room for agency on the part of creatures also explains why the mechanism of the two affections is important. It's not that free choice in general requires open alternatives: God cannot do evil, but he is free and praiseworthy when he does good. But that's because God is the ultimate source of all his own actions. God is *a se*: he does not receive his nature or actions from outside himself. Free choice on the part of creatures does require open alternatives, however, because creatures do receive their natures from outside themselves, from God; if their actions flow by necessity from their natures, those actions are not ultimately theirs, but God's. A free action, one for which the agent can be praised or blamed, has its source within the agent, not outside. The two affections given by God, neither of which determines action, allow the space in which the angels can exercise a causality that is genuinely their own and thus be the source of their own actions.

Now when Anselm said that free choice was not essentially the power to sin or not to sin, God was not his only example of a free being who cannot sin; the good angels are likewise supposed to be free but unable to sin. Though they were originally able to sin, just like the angels who fell, the good angels are no longer able to sin. The reason, Anselm explains, is that as a reward for their retaining justice when they could have abandoned it, God gave them the very 'something more' that they had voluntarily forgone for the sake of justice. Therefore, there is no happiness left for them to desire that they do not already possess, so there is nothing for their affection for happiness to latch on to that could tempt them to abandon justice. Yet they remain free, because they retain—and indeed ceaselessly exercise—the power to preserve justice.

As for the angels who abandoned justice for the sake of that 'something more', not only did they lose justice, but they failed to attain the happiness they sought, and God punished them with grave unhappiness. And because they lack justice, they cannot return to God. They lack rectitude 'irrecoverably'.

Anselm intends this whole account of the fall of the angels as a philosophical analysis of the essential conditions of free choice on the part of a rational being. In short, free choice—and, with it, moral responsibility—are possible only when an agent can be the ultimate source of its own actions. There must be something the agent has that it has not received, whether from God as the creator of its nature, or from heredity and environment as the causes of its belief and desires, or from whatever other external source might be thought to determine its actions.

Human beings are also rational beings—the only rational beings besides angels, as far as Anselm knows—and the same general analysis of free choice applies to us. Christian tradition tells us that our first parents fell by disobeying God, and by applying Anselm's analysis we can conclude that they originally had justice and the power to preserve it, but they abandoned justice for the sake of a happiness that, it turned out, was not theirs to obtain. In this fall they, and not God, were the source of their action.

Like the fallen angels, human beings lack justice and therefore cannot return to God on our own. Unlike the fallen angels, however, we do not lack rectitude 'irrecoverably'. We can be restored to rectitude by divine initiative. Our miraculous creation, spoiled by our voluntary rebellion, can be remade by a miraculous redemption.

Chapter 6
The great restoration project

Anselm's account of the primal choice of the angels is, as I have emphasized, meant as a general account of how any rational being can be the source of its own action, whether for good or for ill. So the basic explanation of the fall of the angels applies equally to the sin of Adam and Eve. From the beginning, Anselm believes, human beings did not 'do the truth'; they freely threw away justice and chose what they thought would make them happy. They thereby missed out on God's purpose for them. But God's purposes do not change, any more than God himself changes; so God is committed, by the very project of creation itself, to restoring human beings to the possibility of knowing and loving him that was his aim in creating them. That possibility is thwarted as long as human beings remain in the state of alienation from God into which the sin of their first parents thrust them. So if God is to be true to himself, and to the generous purpose of his original act of creation, he must rescue human beings from that alienation.

Anselm's greatest legacy to systematic theology is his account of God's great restoration project. In outline, the argument is simple. Sin, Anselm contends, is of infinite seriousness, because it is an affront to the infinite majesty and honour of God. By sinning, our first parents put themselves and all their natural descendants in an intolerable situation: there is nothing any of them can do to pay back the debt, to repair the breach, because even if they could offer everything they are and everything they do, that is no more than they owe God anyway; they cannot restore the balance, satisfy the debt, or repair the breach by their own resources. And God cannot simply dismiss the debt, as if human rebellion were no big deal after all; such moral frivolity would be grossly incompatible with the perfection of the divine character. So God the Son takes the debt on himself by becoming human. He willingly offers his own life as satisfaction for sin. Because his life belongs to one who has a divine nature, it is an infinitely valuable offering, and therefore a more than adequate satisfaction; because he is also a descendant of Adam, he can make the offering as one of the race of debtors, so that the satisfaction is offered by us to God.

The Christian claim that the work of Christ reconciles human beings to God is known as the doctrine of atonement (at-one-ment); Anselm's distinctive account of this doctrine is known as the satisfaction theory of atonement, because of the central role that the notion of satisfaction plays. My brief outline offers only an overview of the satisfaction theory. Several notions in the outline, including that of satisfaction itself, require more elaboration; and the reasons that the satisfaction theory is so hotly contested even to this day also deserve attention. The best way to approach Anselm's theory is to begin with a look at the questions he intends to answer.

The questions

One crucial point about Anselm's account in *Cur Deus Homo* is that it is intended as an answer to particular questions. It is not intended as an answer to just any question one might have about the atonement. So the framing of the question, the particular target of the arguments, has to be taken into account if we are to have any hope of understanding and evaluating Anselm's account.

The arguments to which Anselm's account of atonement is meant as a response are posed as objections from unbelievers by Anselm's interlocutor, Boso. The objections themselves, it appears, were reported to Anselm by his friend Gilbert Crispin, abbot of Westminster, who heard them raised by learned Jews who had recently arrived in London. The first such argument is that the Christian account of redemption portrays God as acting in an unseemly way:

> Unbelievers who deride our simplicity object that we injure and insult God when we say that he descended into a woman's womb, was born of a woman, grew by being nourished by milk and human foods, and (not to mention many other things that do not appear to be suitable for God) suffered fatigue, hunger, thirst, beatings, and crucifixion and death between thieves.

It is an affront to the divine dignity to maintain 'that the Most High should stoop to such lowly things'.

Accordingly, Anselm's first task is to defend the seemliness—the beauty, as he prefers to think of it—of the Christian account of redemption. Anselm replies to Boso:

> We do not injure or insult God at all. On the contrary, we praise and proclaim the ineffable depth of his mercy, giving thanks with our whole hearts.... If [unbelievers] attentively considered how fitting a way this was to accomplish the restoration of humankind, they would not deride our simplicity but join with us in praising God's wise benevolence.

And Anselm proceeds to wax eloquent about the great beauty and glory of the Christian story, the poetic parallels that show how fitting it was for human redemption to be accomplished in the way that Christians say it was.

Boso agrees that the story is beautiful—but that's in part because he thinks it's true. As a way of answering the objections of unbelievers, the appeal to beauty fails, he says:

When someone wants to produce a picture, he chooses something sturdy on which to paint, so that his painting will last. No one paints on water or in the air, since no traces of the picture would remain there. So when we offer unbelievers these instances of what you say is fitting as pictures of an actual fact, they think it is as though we are painting on a cloud, since they hold that what we believe is not an actual fact at all, but a fiction. Therefore, one must first demonstrate the rational solidity of the truth: that is, the necessity that proves that God should or could have humbled himself to the things that we proclaim about him. Only then should one expound on considerations of fittingness as pictures of this truth, so that the body of truth, so to speak, might shine all the more brightly.

In other words, show that the Christian story *must* be true—that God *had* to act as we Christians say he did—and only then will your encomia to the beauty of that story carry conviction.

In this way the answer to the unseemliness objection makes room for Boso to pose, on behalf of unbelievers, the more fundamental objection that occupies the bulk of *Cur Deus Homo*: the objection that the Christian account of redemption portrays God as acting irrationally. It was irrational for God to engage in this elaborate contrivance in order to accomplish a reconciliation that he surely could have accomplished by simple fiat: for do you not say that he is omnipotent? If there was no necessity that he go to all that trouble—if the cup could indeed have passed from Christ with no detriment to humankind—then God acted irrationally by treating Christ, or allowing him to be treated, in the way he did, condemning a just man for the sake of sinners.

It won't do, Boso argues, to say what many of the fathers said: that it was in fact necessary for God to do this because the devil had certain rights over humanity that God had to respect. For God remains sovereign even over sinful creatures. Both the devil and human beings are still God's own possession; God retains his prerogative to do as he pleases 'with his own, about his own, in his own'. So although human beings deserved to be punished, and it was appropriate for the devil to punish them, God had every right to remove human beings from the devil's jurisdiction. The devil had acquired no rights over human beings; far from deserving to punish them, he deserved to be punished along with them.

So (the unbeliever concludes) in the absence of any plausible reason to think that the death of Christ was necessary for human redemption, the Christian account of redemption portrays God as acting irrationally. In order to answer this objection, Anselm undertakes to show that reconciliation between God and humanity could *only* take place through the voluntary self-offering of a being who is both fully divine and fully human. That is, the passion and death of Christ were *necessary* for human redemption. Thus, no charge of irrationality lies against God for securing human redemption in that way, for there was no other way in which he could have secured it.

The answer, and how Anselm conceives his task in *Cur Deus Homo*

Thus, the question that Anselm sets out to answer is 'How, on the Christian account of redemption, can God's rationality be defended?' And for reasons that we have now seen, he interprets this question as asking why God *had* to redeem humanity in the way Christians say he did. The answer to this question—the conclusion that *Cur Deus Homo* is dedicated to establishing—is that it is not possible for God to save humanity without becoming incarnate and dying for our sins. But there is a further point, never explicitly raised as a question but nonetheless answered at considerable length. The unbeliever's objection in effect assumes that if human beings are in need of saving, God has to save them; the objection is simply that on the Christian account of human redemption, God secures human salvation in an irrational and unseemly manner. Suppose, however, that Anselm can prove that

God cannot save humanity without becoming incarnate and dying. It is still open to the unbeliever to say that in that case, it would have been seemlier and more reasonable for God to have left human beings unsaved, rather than subjecting himself to pain and human death in order to secure their salvation. Anselm must therefore argue not only that God can secure human salvation only through the death of a God-man but also that if human beings fall into sin, God cannot simply leave them unsaved.

We may state the required argument in the following form:

> (1) Necessarily, if human beings sin, God offers them reconciliation.
> (2) Necessarily, if God does not become incarnate and die, God does not offer reconciliation to human beings.
> Therefore, (3) Necessarily, if human beings sin, God becomes incarnate and dies.

Anselm attempts to make this argument '*remoto Christo*', that is, without appeal to any of the details of the Christian story, for the unbelievers who are the targets of the argument do not accept that story.

Now one might well think that the quest to establish by reason alone that God has to become incarnate and die for the redemption of humanity is quixotic in the extreme. But it's important to acknowledge that this is what Anselm sets out to do.

Anselm's case for his answer

Both of the premises in the key argument of *Cur Deus Homo* require defence, and Anselm makes his case for each of them piecemeal. Rather than following Anselm's order of presentation, I will organize his arguments in a more linear fashion—though I will begin, as Anselm also does, with the defence of premise (2), the claim that, necessarily, sinful human beings are reconciled to God only through the death of a God-man. Anselm first argues that reconciliation requires satisfaction. That is, God does not—he cannot, as a matter of justice—simply cancel the debt of sin. Rather, the debt must be paid, either by way of punishment or by way of satisfaction.

Although it is customary and perfectly proper to translate Anselm's *debitum* as 'debt', it is also important not to press the commercial analogy so far that Anselm's picture of the relationship of human beings to God appears needlessly crude. What human beings owe God is simply what they ought to do. The verb *debere* may equally well be translated 'owe' and 'ought', and a *debitum* can be either a debt in the commercial sense or an obligation in a broader legal or moral sense. It is true that the breadth of meaning of these words allows Anselm to switch back and forth between the language of commercial transactions and the language of justice and obligation, but we should not be tempted to think that Anselm regards justice as a kind of commercial exchange in which God acts as a rather obsessive auditor who insists that the books be balanced down to the last farthing. Rather, if we must press a differentiation to which Anselm's language does not really lend itself, it is better to say that for Anselm, debt is a species of obligation and can therefore serve as an illuminating analogy for our relationship to God. Something similar can be said about the much-maligned feudal character of the notion of 'honour', which Anselm also uses in this section. Accordingly, one cannot immediately dismiss Anselm's doctrine simply because one regards as crude or antiquated the metaphors he uses in developing it.

In fact, for Anselm the notions of *dishonouring God* and of *failing to pay what one owes God* are interdefinable not only with each other but also with the notion of *sinning*, which is a notion that few Christian theologians will regard as dispensable. In Book I, chapter 11, he makes the connections among these three notions quite clear:

> Every will of a rational creature ought to be subject to God's
> will....This is the debt that human beings and angels owe to God.
> No one who discharges this debt sins, and everyone who fails to
> discharge it sins. This is the justice or rectitude of will that makes
> people just or upright in heart, that is, in will. This is the only and
> the complete honour that we owe God or that God requires of
> us....Someone who does not pay back to God the honour that is
> owed him takes from God what is rightly his and dishonours God;
> and this is what sinning is.

Consequently, Anselm can offer two independent arguments for
the claim that God cannot simply forgive sins 'by mercy alone'.
The argument of Book I, chapter 12, relies primarily (though only
obliquely) on the metaphor of debt, that of chapter 13 primarily
(and quite explicitly) on the metaphor of honour, but they come to
the same thing in the end. God would act unjustly if he made no
distinction between the sinful and the just, requiring neither
satisfaction nor punishment for sin, leaving uncorrected the
disorder that sin introduces, and acquiescing in the intolerable
refusal of rational creatures to subject themselves to God's will as
they ought to do. Since God cannot act unjustly, sin must be
followed by either punishment or satisfaction.

Now if sin is simply punished, the demands of justice are met; but
human beings are not reconciled with God. And what God wants,
according to Anselm, is to restore the relationship that human sin
has breached. So punishment would be entirely beside the point.
Reconciliation requires satisfaction. *Satisfactio* is, literally, 'doing
enough': the word is used in ordinary Latin for reparation or
amends. Satisfaction, as Anselm understands it, is a recompense
that heals the breach between God and human beings, an
adequate repayment for the debt of sin, sufficient amends for the
affront of dishonouring God.

The argument to this point establishes that reconciliation requires
satisfaction. In order to defend (2), Anselm must argue further

that only the death of a God-man can serve as satisfaction. Anselm argues that even the most apparently trivial sin is of infinite gravity and therefore requires an infinite satisfaction. He asks Boso to imagine that he finds himself under God's watchful eye. Someone tells Boso, 'Look over there', but God says he doesn't want Boso to look. Anselm asks Boso whether he would take that glance, contrary to the expressed will of God. Boso says he would not do so for any consideration: not to save his own life, not to keep the entire world from destruction, not even to preserve an infinite number of worlds 'as full of creatures as this one is'. Anselm draws the disheartening conclusion: 'That is how seriously we sin every time we knowingly do something, however small, contrary to the will of God; for we are always under his watchful eye, and he always commands us not to sin'. Every sin, in short, is infinitely serious and therefore requires a satisfaction of infinite value.

Anselm then argues that only a God-man can make satisfaction for human sin. The one who makes the satisfaction must be a human being, since only a human being can pay what human beings owe. (An overly literal reading of the commercial metaphor will make a hash of Anselm's point, since it is not in general true that only the person who owes a debt can discharge it. We all know that if Jane gets into financial trouble, Beth can bail her out. What Anselm is getting at is that sin ruins the proper relationship between God and humanity. Unless there is some change *in humanity*, the breach in that relationship does not get healed.) Yet only God can make this satisfaction, since the satisfaction must be proportionate to the sin, which is infinitely serious; and only God can give something of his own that is of infinite value. Therefore, the one who makes the satisfaction must be both divine and human. And the divine and human natures must come together into a single being:

> If... these two intact natures are said to be conjoined in such a way that the human being is distinct from God, and it is not one and the

same being that is both God and human, it is impossible for the two of them to do what needs to be done. God will not do it, because he will not owe the debt; the human being will not do it, because he will not be able to. Therefore, in order for the God-man to do this, it is necessary that the one who is going to make this satisfaction be both perfect God and perfect man, since only one who is truly God can make it, but only one who is truly human owes it. Therefore, since it is necessary that a God-man be found, one who preserves both natures intact, it is no less necessary that these intact natures come together into one person, just as a body and a rational soul come together into one human being. There is no other way for one and the same being to be perfect God and perfect man.

In short, only a God-man can make the satisfaction that God cannot fail to offer.

So now Anselm has established the necessity of a God-man, but he has not quite finished the argument for (2), because he has not yet shown that the God-man makes satisfaction *by dying*. We have already seen that the God-man must make satisfaction by giving God something 'greater than everything that is less than God'. Anselm argues that this satisfaction must be either the God-man himself or something belonging to him, since nothing below him or outside him is great enough to serve as a satisfaction. Moreover, the satisfaction must be something that God cannot demand of the God-man as an obligation: 'he will lay down himself or something of his own for the honour of God in a way that he is not obligated to do'. Now because the God-man will be sinless, he will not be obligated to die, though he will have the power to lay down his life if he chooses. So he can make satisfaction by laying down his life for the honour of God.

This completes the argument for (2), so we can turn to the argument for (1), the claim that, necessarily, if human beings sin, God offers them reconciliation. It is evident, Anselm says, that 'God made rational nature just, in order that it might be happy in enjoying him'. And rationality, for Anselm, is simply the power 'to discern the just from what is not just, the true from what is not true, the good from what is not good, and the greater good from the lesser good'. Rational nature receives this power of discernment in order to choose according to its dictates:

> Otherwise God would have given it this power of discernment in vain, since its discernment would be in vain if it did not love and avoid things in accordance with its discernment; and it is not fitting that God should bestow so great a power in vain. And so it is certain that rational nature was made for the purpose of loving and choosing the supreme good above all other things, not for the sake of something else, but for his own sake. After all, if rational nature loves the supreme good for the sake of something else, it loves something else and not the supreme good. Now it cannot love the supreme good for its own sake unless it is just. Therefore, it was made rational and just at the same time so that it would not be rational in vain.

Given that rational nature was made rational and just, in order to love the supreme good above all other things and for its own sake, we can conclude further that God intended rational nature to be happy. Otherwise, we would have to say that a rational nature that loved the supreme good above all else but was perpetually estranged from that very good was achieving its God-given purpose. But it is absurd, Anselm says, to think that God's gift of rationality and justice will be, by God's own design, permanently deprived of its proper fulfilment. We can conclude, then, that human beings, as rational creatures, were 'made just in order that [they] might be happy in enjoying the supreme good, that is, God'.

God's purpose for rational nature does not change simply because human beings have thrown away the justice with which they were created. So if God were to leave human beings in a state of injustice and unhappiness, he would fail in his purpose; he would have created human beings in vain:

> it is utterly foreign to [God] that he should allow any rational nature to perish entirely.... It is therefore necessary that he complete what he began in human nature. And as we have said, this can take place only through a perfect satisfaction for sin, which no sinner can make.

Therefore, since God cannot fail in his purpose for rational nature, 'which he created so that it might rejoice in him', a perfect satisfaction for sin must be made available; and that perfect satisfaction is the voluntary self-offering of the Incarnate Word.

Note: it must be a *voluntary* self-offering. If Christ's death is a violent death, in the sense of a death unwillingly sustained, it is unavailing for the purpose of reconciliation. The cause of the alienation between God and humanity is in us, not in God; the remedy therefore requires a change in us. The offering on the part of humanity—on the part of Christ as our representative—must well up from our own purposes and desires, which is to say, from Christ's own will. And (to look at the same thing from the side of Christ's divine nature) it is because of God's character—because God, in the unshakable firmness of his loving purpose for humanity, cannot allow the project of creation to come to nothing—that the reconciliation must be offered; and God's will for humanity is not the Father's will, imposed upon the Son, but the united will of all the Divine Persons, one of whom graciously and willingly becomes flesh in order that he may both carry out the divine purpose and effect the needed change in humanity.

Anselm accordingly emphasizes Jesus's own initiative and spends two whole chapters of *Cur Deus Homo* explaining how we are to read Scriptural passages that might suggest passivity, reluctance, or compulsion on Christ's part. The true character of Christ's sovereign and free self-offering is best captured, for Anselm, in words Jesus speaks in the Fourth Gospel:

> I am laying down my life in order that I might take it up again. No one is taking it from me, but I am laying it down of my own accord. I have the power to lay it down, and I have the power to take it up again.

The satisfaction theory and some common misunderstandings

Anselm's theory of atonement can be summed up in a single sentence:

> The voluntary self-offering of the infinitely precious life of the God-man repairs the infinite breach that sin had opened up between God and humanity and thereby restores the possibility of eternal happiness that God intended for humanity in creation.

Granted, this statement expresses his account without employing the metaphors that Anselm uses in developing it. But it does so without the loss of anything essential to the view, and indeed it thereby opens up possibilities for contemporary thinkers to express the same view using metaphors and imagery that might speak more compellingly today.

The satisfaction theory of atonement remains highly contested. It is not my task here either to defend it (beyond giving it a sympathetic exposition) or to criticize it, but I do think it is helpful to clarify some features of the view by addressing common misconceptions that one often sees both in the scholarly literature and in more popular accounts. First, it is often mischaracterized as a form of penal substitutionary atonement. On a penal substitution view, Christ atones for human sin by taking the punishment for sin in our place. Anselm's account, however, is not penal: Christ's death is in no sense a punishment, and punishment would not serve God's redemptive purpose. Nor is Anselm's account substitutionary. Christ does not suffer in our stead, but for our sake. The difference may seem slight, but to Anselm it is crucial. His view is not that God the Father does something to Christ instead of doing it to us, but that Christ does something on our behalf that we cannot do for ourselves.

Another common mischaracterization is that Anselm's account of atonement is unduly focused on blood and suffering. This is a particularly strange misreading, since, given the task Anselm sets himself, nothing in his account can depend on the historical details of Christ's death; neither blood nor the Cross, as such, plays any role. And even when the historical reality of Christ's death is in view (outside *Cur Deus Homo*), Anselm's attention is occupied almost entirely by its redemptive efficacy and not by its gore.

Finally, contrary to some critics, Anselm's account does not glorify violence or justify further violence. Christ lays down his life of his own accord; a violent death, in the sense of a death unwillingly sustained, would be of no redemptive value. And nothing in Anselm's account justifies violence against human beings. Christ's suffering has redemptive efficacy because his life is infinitely precious (being the life of a person who has a divine nature) and he lays it down of his own accord. Suffering unwillingly sustained, or sustained by someone whose life is not infinitely precious (as is the case for every merely human person), is of no redemptive value and can find no justification in Anselm.

Chapter 7
Living in the meantime

The atoning work of Christ is, as one liturgist deeply influenced by Anselm put it, 'a full, perfect, and sufficient sacrifice, oblation, and satisfaction for the sins of the whole world'. At its root, to satisfy—*satisfacere*—is to do enough, to accomplish what is sufficient. The sufficiency of the atonement means that no further offering needs to be made to God in order to restore God's honour and heal the breach that human sin has made between God and humanity: but it does not mean that the effects of the sin of our first parents are automatically wiped away or that we can now coast on the infinite worth of the God-man's self-offering and go on doing whatever we like. We must accept the rescue, claim the benefits that are made available through Christ's death, and turn again and again away from mere advantage and towards justice.

Satisfaction and salvation

Near the end of *Cur Deus Homo* Anselm considers explicitly, albeit briefly, how the cosmic satisfaction achieved by the death of the God-man is made effective in individual lives. By freely offering his life for the honour of God and the redemption of humanity, Christ earns a great reward. But the reward cannot be given to Christ himself, who, being God, is in need of nothing. So, Anselm says, God gives the reward to those whom Christ chooses:

To whom will Christ more fittingly give the fruit and reward of his death than to those for whose salvation he made himself a human being, as truthful reasoning has taught us, and to whom, as we have said, he gave an example by dying for the sake of justice? For their imitation of him will be unavailing if they do not share in what he has earned. And whom will he more justly make heirs of the reward he does not need, and of the abundance of his own riches, than his own kindred and siblings, whom he sees languishing in poverty and deep misery, bound by their many and great debts, so that what they owe for their sin is forgiven and they are given what they lack on account of their sins?

Boso replies:

The world can hear nothing more reasonable, nothing sweeter, nothing more desirable. For my part, this gives birth to such assurance in me that I can no longer express the great joy with which my heart exults. For it seems to me that God rejects no one who approaches him under this name.

Boso's outburst of joy exemplifies the sunny, confident side of Anselm's portrayal of life in the meantime, life between satisfaction and ultimate consummation. But there is a demanding, anxious, even anguished side as well, and it is important to look at those elements in order to get the complete picture.

In the treatises the blight of sin and its consequences, if it appears at all, gives way in due time to the good news of insight and grace. The *Proslogion* opens with an anguished address to God by one who describes himself as wretched, exiled from God, and bereft of the knowledge of God for which he was created; but by the end of the work he has come to understand that than which a greater cannot be thought; he is contemplating the overwhelming joys of heaven and praying that he 'might grow day by day until my joy comes to fullness'. *Cur Deus Homo* dwells on the infinite seriousness of even the smallest sin but argues ultimately for the infinite generosity of divine mercy. The exacting demands of discipleship are much more evident in Anselm's letters, prayers, and meditations (see Figure 3).

The demands of discipleship

At perhaps the opposite pole from the cheerful confidence in divine grace that we find in the treatises is Anselm's second meditation, 'A lament for virginity unhappily lost'. The clearly genuine horror with which Anselm regards his sexual sin, and the torment that he does not merely express but actively seeks to intensify, make for very difficult reading:

> Miserable little man, cast yourself headlong into the dark abyss of boundless grief, for it was by your own will that you were cast down into a pit of horrifying wickedness. Be buried, wretched man, under the terrible weight of sorrow, for you delighted to sink into the filth and stench of hell. Wrap yourself, you miserable man, in the terrifying darkness of unassuageable grief, for you were willing to throw yourself into the whirlpool of such sordid lust. Plunge into the raging abyss of bitterness, because you took pleasure in wallowing in wickedness.
>
> O fear that makes me shudder, sorrow that makes me fear, grief beyond all consolation: heap yourselves upon me! Attack me, bury me, disquiet me, entangle me, take possession of me!

Near the end of the prayer he takes comfort in God's assurance that 'I do not desire the death of a sinner' and throws himself on the mercy of God; but the atmosphere of the prayer never lightens entirely, and the best he can manage to say at the end is that it is not out of the question that God might spare him: 'it is not impossible for your omnipotence, or unsuitable to your justice, or unaccustomed for your mercy. For "you are good, for your mercy is everlasting", you who are blessed forever. Amen'.

3. Anselm hands over a book of his *Prayers* to his friend Matilda of Tuscany.

The 'Lament for virginity unhappily lost' is early (probably written in the early 1070s) and somewhat atypical, but Anselm never loses the sense that life in the meantime is lived on a knife-edge between heaven and hell. In a letter to Basilia, widow of the Norman magnate Hugh of Gournay, Anselm describes our earthly life as one in which we are always going either upward or downward (for an excerpt, see the box entitled 'Letter to Basilia (*c*.1099)'. We must be perpetually alert to which path we are taking; there is no assurance that our upward path—if we are even on an upward path—will continue from one moment to the next. Although the letter was written around 1099, near Basilia's death, Anselm placed it at the end of his collection of letters as archbishop, ten years later. Perhaps, as the eminent historian Sally Vaughn suggests, 'the nearness of his own death made his memory of her death seem to suggest its relevance there'; but perhaps also he recognized in the letter an apt summary of the spiritual counsel he had been offering for nearly sixty years.

Grace and free choice

Anselm urges Basilia to recoil from sin and employ herself in holy acts as much as she can 'with God's help'. Without the help of God's grace, no right action is possible. Grace belongs to the miraculous course of events—those that take place by God's will alone—rather than the natural or the voluntary. Nevertheless, Anselm argues, grace is not in conflict with free choice. He devotes the third question of *De concordia* to the harmony of divine grace and human free choice.

The question arises, he says, because of the apparently conflicting testimony of Scripture: 'in some places Scripture speaks in such a way that it seems free choice is unavailing for salvation and grace does everything, whereas in other places it speaks as if the whole of our salvation rests on our own free will'. For example, in one passage Jesus says, 'Without me you can do nothing'; yet in another he seems to appeal to our free choice to respond to him:

Letter to Basilia (c.1099)

I will tell you something, most dearly beloved daughter, that will be able to enkindle your heart fiercely towards fear of God and love of a good life if you will meditate on it again and again with all your attention. Let it be always before the eyes of your mind that this present life comes to an end, and no one knows when its last day, to which we grow ever nearer, day and night, will come. This present life is a journey, and as long as we human beings are alive, we are doing nothing but walking that path. We are always either going up or going down: going up into heaven, or else going down into hell. When someone does a good deed, she takes one step upward; but when someone sins in any way, she takes one step downward. This upward or downward path becomes known to each soul when it departs the body. Someone who zealously strives, so long as she is living here, to go upward by means of good conduct and good works will be welcomed to her place in heaven alongside the good angels; but one who goes downward through bad conduct and bad deeds will be cast into hell with the fallen angels. It should indeed be kept in mind that one goes downward much more quickly and much more easily than upward. Hence, in all their wills and in all their actions Christian men and women ought to consider attentively whether they are going upward or downward, and to embrace wholeheartedly those in which they see they are going upward, and to flee and abhor like hell itself those in which they recognize the downward path. And so I admonish and counsel you, dearest friend and daughter in Christ, to recoil from any sin, great or small, and to employ yourself in holy acts, as much as you can with God's help.

'Come to me, all you who labor and are burdened, and I will
refresh you. Take my yoke upon you and learn from me, for I am
gentle and lowly of heart, and you will find rest for your souls'.
Some claim to prove from experience that there is no free choice:
they observe that people make enormous efforts towards spiritual
progress but make no progress at all, or fall away from the
progress they have made with no hope of recovery. Yet the justice
of God in repaying both the good and the wicked according to
their deserts surely makes sense only on the assumption that there
is free choice.

The question at issue is grace and free choice as they relate to
salvation in those who have attained the use of reason. (Baptized
infants who die before they attain the use of reason do not have
the opportunity to exercise their free choice; they are saved by
grace alone.) Those who are saved are saved on account of justice,
which is rectitude of will preserved for its own sake. And the only
way a creature can have rectitude of will in the first place is for
God to give it: this giving of rectitude is precisely God's grace. The
creature can then preserve rectitude of will through free choice.

The initial gift of grace is entirely unmerited, but 'the will, by
preserving through free choice what it has received, [can merit]
an increase of the justice it has received'; such an increase of
justice will be a fruit of the first grace and therefore 'grace for
grace'. Grace can increase the intensity of justice in the will, so that
one clings to rectitude of will more strongly and the power of
temptation is weakened. It can also increase the extent of justice,
so that one comes to be just in some new domain, as a person who
is temperate with respect to drink might be given the additional
grace of chastity. But Anselm says that salvation is promised, not
to all those who possess some justice, but only to those whose
justice is complete. 'It is not part of our aim here to show how a
human being comes to be free from all injustice', he says, 'but
we do know that this is possible for a Christian through holy efforts
and through God's grace'.

The justice brought about by grace remains in the will unless the will abandons it by willing something incompatible with grace: 'for example, someone receives the rectitude of willing sobriety and then throws it away by willing immoderate pleasure from drinking'. Temptation can never overpower a just will, Anselm says; what people sometimes describe as the impossibility of upholding rectitude of will is not really impossibility, just difficulty—sometimes, admittedly, severe difficulty.

Those who are just will what they ought to will, because they ought to will it (rather than for the sake of impressing other people or avoiding punishment or what have you). But this abstract account of justice does not, by itself, tell us very much about the shape of life in the meantime: we need an account of what we ought to will. Anselm never really lays out a systematic ethical theory, but there are certain prominent themes in his writings—both in his treatises and in the pastoral advice he offers in his letters—that give us a reasonably good picture of how he understood the demands of justice.

How can we live justly?

Anselm says that 'for any will that preserves rectitude, its preserving rectitude for the sake of rectitude itself is the same as its willing what God wills it to will'. Anselm speaks in his letters as if knowing what God wants us to will is pretty straightforward. Writing to Robert and his small community of Anglo-Saxon nuns in the autumn of 1106, Anselm says:

> If you want to know what will of yours is righteous, a will that is subject to the will of God is unquestionably righteous. So when you are planning or thinking about doing anything, great or small, speak thus within your hearts: 'Does God will that I will this, or not?' If your conscience answers, 'God truly wills that I will this, and such a will is pleasing to him', then love that will of yours, no

matter whether you can carry it out or not. But if your conscience
bears witness to you that God does not will that you have that will,
then turn your heart away from it with all your might; and if you
truly want to drive that will away from you, banish from your heart,
insofar as you can, even the thought and the memory of it.

Here Anselm makes discerning God's will seem extraordinarily
simple. We just consult our conscience, the internal witness to
God's will. If we encounter difficulties in willing or acting as God
wants us to, the problem will not be ignorance, but wayward
desires that make it difficult (though of course never impossible)
to will as we know we ought to will.

Occasionally, however, people do suffer from genuine ignorance of
God's will, or at least difficulty in discerning it. When we have a
strong desire for one course of action, we are likely to weigh
alternatives incorrectly:

whenever we set out to choose from a number of possibilities the
one that we ought to, we should set aside every desire of our own
and consider only the weight of the things themselves. If we join the
weight of love to the weight of the thing loved, our judgement in
distinguishing things will inevitably go astray.

It is also possible for corrupt customs to cloud our judgement.
One of the reasons Anselm was so keen on calling a primatial
council, as he was finally able to do in September 1102 with
the cooperation of Henry I, was to enact strict legislation
against sodomy. 'One must bear in mind', Anselm observed,
'that up to now this sin has been so common that hardly
anyone was ashamed of it, and for that reason many heedlessly
gave themselves over to it without realizing how serious a sin
it is'. Once the council has spoken, however, no one can plead
ignorance; violating the expressed will of the church is outright
disobedience and merits punishment accordingly.

It would be hard to overstate the centrality of obedience in Anselm's thinking and in the conduct of his own life. When Anselm became aware of the prohibition on lay investiture, he immediately understood it as his duty to stamp out the practice in England, even though he had accepted it before and (as far as anyone can tell) never really examined or cared about the rationale behind the prohibition. He cautioned monks and nuns to obey their superiors not only in their outward deeds but in their wills, even to the point of imagining that their very thoughts are open to their superiors: 'Let your heart be always open to your abbot, and wherever you may be, reckon that not only your body but also your thoughts are before his eyes: and then do and think what you would not be embarrassed to do and think in his presence'. No act of disobedience, however apparently small, is insignificant: 'disobedience by itself banished human beings from paradise'.

Not all authority is benign, as Anselm knew from bitter experience, and we must not obey human authority when doing so would oppose the will of God. Beyond this important qualification, however, obedience is not only intrinsically right but also beneficial in its consequences. In much the same way that faithfulness to Christian doctrine sets one free to explore the reason of faith without the risk of intellectual shipwreck, obedience provides a context in which one can lead a just life in as much tranquillity as conditions this side of Eden permit. The peace and good order that obedience establishes mirror the perfect order established by God in creation, an order both supremely wise and supremely beautiful; in that order human beings take our rightful place in creation and fulfil God's purpose for us.

The essence of life in the meantime

'As yet I am halfway between fear and hope in serving God', Anselm says in his Prayer to the Holy Cross: perhaps as apt a

Chronology

1100	William II dies, succeeded by Henry I; Anselm returns to England
1102	Completes *On the Procession of the Holy Spirit*
1103–6	Second exile: away from England because of conflict with Henry I
1106	Returns to England
1107–8	Completes *De concordia*
1109	Dies at Canterbury on 21 April

Anselm

References

References to Anselm's works are given using the following abbreviations: AR, Anselm's Reply to Gaunilo; CDH, *Cur Deus Homo*; DC, *De concordia*; DCD, *De casu diaboli* (*On the Fall of the Devil*); DCV, *De conceptu virginali, et de originali peccato* (*On the Virginal Conception, and On Original Sin*); DIV, *De incarnatione Verbi* (*On the Incarnation of the Word*); DLA, *De libertate arbitrii* (*On Freedom of Choice*); DV, *De veritate* (*On Truth*); M, *Monologion*; P, *Proslogion*; RBF, Gaunilo's 'Reply on Behalf of the Fool'. The abbreviated title is followed by the (book and) chapter number, and then the page number of my own translation in *Anselm: The Complete Treatises* (Indianapolis, IN: Hackett Publishing Company, 2022). References within a single paragraph of the text are combined into a single entry.

Chapter 1: Anselm's life, work, and contexts

R. W. Southern, *Anselm: A Portrait in Landscape* (Cambridge: Cambridge University Press, 1990), 17.

Ibid.

1 Corinthians 2:10.

DIV 1, 226. This language appears not only in the final version of the work that Anselm circulated in 1094 but also in the abandoned first draft he began around 1090.

Letter 77 (i.68.3), 452–3, written sometime between late 1075 and early 1078.

The Scriptural passage quoted in Anselm's letter to Henry is Romans 14:8.

P 25, 115.

Sandra Visser and Thomas Williams, *Anselm* (Oxford: Oxford University Press, 2009), 13–14.

Sally R. Vaughn, *Anselm of Bec and Robert of Meulan: The Innocence of the Dove and the Wisdom of the Serpent* (Berkeley, CA: University of California Press, 1987), 75.

Ibid., 130.

Eadmer, *Historia novorum* 43, quoted in Vaughn, 171. Vaughn points out that £2,000 was roughly 'the annual value of all Canterbury lands and would thus have had much the same effect on the royal treasury as if Rufus had extended the Canterbury vacancy an additional year' (171n.).

Eadmer, *Historia novorum* 72–3, quoted in Vaughn, 189.

Ibid., 78, quoted in Vaughn, 199.

Southern, *Anselm*, 281.

Eadmer, *Vita Anselmi* 66 (Southern, *LA*, 142); ibid. (143).

Chapter 2: Looking at God

M 1, 28; ibid.

P 1, 100; P 2, 100.

Psalms 14:1 and 53:1 (13:1 and 52:1 in the Vulgate).

P 2, 100.

AR 8, 128–9.

M 2, 30.

M 22, 54.

Boethius, *The Consolation of Philosophy*, trans. P. G. Walsh. Oxford World's Classics (Oxford: Oxford University Press, 2008).

DC 1.7, 406.

P 8, 104. The Latin for 'not afflicted with any feeling of compassion for sorrow' is *nulla miseriae compassione afficeris*. This is a particularly deft bit of writing: the verb *afficio*, here in the passive voice, is used both of causing an emotional reaction (hence 'affect') and of afflicting (in the way that someone is said to be afflicted by disease or misfortune). For God to share emotionally in another's sorrow would be a divine misfortune in which God would be passive rather than active.

P 6, 84. Divine mercy is a far more important theme in Anselm's treatises than divine impassibility, with some sixty appearances of the word *misericordia* or *misericors* throughout the corpus, as compared with just eight in two short passages for *impassibilis*.

Mercy is a pervasive theme in the prayers and meditations, and frequent also in the letters.

P 9, 104–5.

Ibid., 105.

P 11, 106; P 11, 107.

Chapter 3: Looking for God

Psalms 14:1 and 53:1 (13:1 and 52:1 in the Vulgate).

P prol., 96.

Ibid. Anselm tells of his struggle in the Prologue to the *Proslogion*; his biographer Eadmer gives a fuller and more dramatic version in *Vita Anselmi* xix (Eadmer, pp. 28–31).

RBF 6, 120. Gaunilo does not formulate his argument with precision, and I go on to state it in such a way that it is more clearly a parallel to Anselm's argument (as Gaunilo understood it). Oddly, despite Gaunilo's sloppy formulation, everyone agrees on what his argument is meant to be, whereas there is endless debate about how to interpret Anselm's.

RG 1, 122.

Ibid.

RG 1, 123.

P prol., 96.

P 3, 101; ibid.

P 2, 100.

P 5, 102.

Chapter 4: How things got started

M 7, 36. It would be more straightforward to argue from the fact that God is immaterial, but Anselm has not yet established that point in the *Monologion*—it comes many chapters later in the 'chaining together of many arguments'—and he is careful about not assuming anything he has yet to prove.

M 9, 38.

M 10, 39.

Ibid.

M 12, 41.

Genesis 1:3; Psalm 33:9 (32:9); Psalm 33:6 (32:6); John 1:1–3. All translations are from the Latin Vulgate.

M 42, 70; ibid.

Prayer to Saint Paul, 518.

M 12, 41; M 30, 61.

Augustine, *De diversis quaestionibus 83*, q. 46.2.

M 31, 62.

DV 2, 134.

DV 5, 139.

Chapter 5: How things went wrong

DCV 11, 343.

DV 12, 150.

Ibid.

DV 12, 151.

This definition first appears at DV 12, 152. Anselm uses it consistently
thereafter in his discussions of justice and freedom in DLA, CDH,
DCV, and DC.

DLA 1, 159.

Ibid.

DCD 1, 179.

DCD 4, 188.

DCD 5, 189.

DCD 12, 198.

DC 3.11, 423.

DCD 13, 204.

DLA 14, 177.

Chapter 6: The great restoration project

Boso was a monk of Bec for whose intellectual abilities Anselm had
particularly high regard. When Anselm went to Canterbury as
archbishop, he summoned Boso there to be an intellectual
companion; Anselm's treatise *On the Virginal Conception, and On
Original Sin*, a companion piece to *Cur Deus Homo*, is addressed
to Boso.

CDH I.3, 252.

CDH I.8, 257.

CDH I.3, 252.

CDH I.4, 252–3.

CDH I.7, 255. Various versions of the theory of the devil's rights appear
in such luminaries as Gregory of Nyssa, Augustine, Leo the Great,
and Gregory the Great. The particular version Boso argues against

was that of the school of Laon, which Southern describes as 'the most respected and responsible school of [Anselm's] day' (203).

CDH I.11, 265.

CDH I.21, 285. Boso comments, 'As I hear it, we are living very dangerously'.

CDH II.7, 298.

CDH II.11, 305.

CDH II.1, 293.

M 68, 88; CDH II.1, 293; ibid.

CDH II.4, 295; ibid.

John 10:17–18, quoted at CDH I.10, 263, and alluded to at CDH II.11, 305, and II.17, 320.

Chapter 7: Living in the meantime

Thomas Cranmer, in the *Book of Common Prayer* 1549 and many subsequent editions.

CDH II.19, 325–6; ibid., 326.

P 26, 116.

Meditatio II, translated from Schmitt III:81; Ezekiel 33:1; Meditatio II, III:81, quoting Psalm 118:1 (117:1).

Sally Vaughn, *St Anselm and the Handmaidens of God: A Study of Anselm's Correspondence with Women* (Turnhout: Brepols, 2003), 94.

DC 3.1, 409–10; John 15:5; Matthew 11:28–9.

DC 3.3, 413; ibid., quoting John 1:16.

DC 3.4, 413; ibid., 414.

DLA 8, 171.

Letter 414, 492.

Letter 193.

Letter 17 (i. 15), 483; Letter 257.

Letter 232, 489; Letter 403, 491.

Prayer to the Holy Cross, 506.

Further reading

Anselm's work in English translation

For all of Anselm's treatises in English, along with a selection of other writings, see T. Williams, *Anselm: The Complete Treatises, with Selected Letters and Prayers and the Meditation on Human Redemption* (Indianapolis, IN: Hackett Publishing Company, 2022). B. Ward, *The Prayers and Meditations of Saint Anselm with the Proslogion* (New York: Penguin Classics, 1979), offers an idiomatic if rather free translation of all of the prayers and meditations. For the complete collection of letters, see W. Fröhlich, *The Letters of Saint Anselm of Canterbury* (Kalamazoo, MI: Cistercian Publications, 1990–4; 3 vols.).

General studies

B. Davies and B. Leftow, eds., *The Cambridge Companion to Anselm* (Cambridge: Cambridge University Press, 2004) presents a comprehensive overview of Anselm's philosophy and theology, comprising twelve essays by leading scholars. For a chronological treatment of the whole of Anselm's work, see E. Sweeney, *Anselm of Canterbury and the Desire for the Word* (Washington, DC: The Catholic University of America Press, 2012). Sweeney argues that Anselm's whole corpus 'is a single project in which knowledge of God and knowledge of self are inextricably linked'; the project is a 'union of the self with God' (p. 7). By contrast, S. Visser and T. Williams, *Anselm* (Oxford: Oxford University Press, 2008), is organized thematically rather than chronologically; this study is particularly distinctive for its account of faith seeking understanding, its reading of Anselm's arguments for the existence of God, and its treatment of Anselm's Christology and soteriology.

Chapter 1: Anselm's life, work, and contexts

T. J. Holopainen, *Dialectic and Theology in the Eleventh Century* (Leiden: Brill, 1996), is essential reading on the 11th-century revival of dialectic and the controversies it generated. Holopainen examines Peter Damian, Lanfranc of Bec, Berengar of Tours, and Anselm. The biography of Anselm written by his pupil and disciple Eadmer is presented in Latin and English on facing pages in R. W. Southern, *The Life of St Anselm, Archbishop of Canterbury, by Eadmer* (Oxford: Oxford University Press, 1962). The indispensable modern biography remains R. W. Southern, *Saint Anselm: A Portrait in Landscape* (Cambridge: Cambridge University Press, 1990). Southern is sensitive to the whole range of Anselm's writings and to his intellectual context. S. N. Vaughn, *Anselm of Bec and Robert of Meulan: The Innocence of the Dove and the Wisdom of the Serpent* (Berkeley, CA: University of California Press, 1987), examines the relationship between Anselm and Count Robert of Meulan, who was Anselm's principal political adversary under the two English kings under whom Anselm served as archbishop of Canterbury. Vaughn gives Anselm credit for a good deal more political savvy than Southern does; her account of Anselm's role in the investiture controversy in particular provides useful balance.

Chapter 2: Looking at God

Sandra Visser and I devote a chapter to the divine attributes in *Anselm* (Oxford: Oxford University Press, 2009), pp. 95–122; and Brian Leftow's essay, 'Anselm's Perfect Being Theology', in Davies and Leftow, *The Cambridge Companion to Anselm*, pp. 132–56, is very useful. For the best way into the debate over Anselm's view of time, see first Katherin Rogers's defence of an eternalist reading in 'Anselmian Eternalism: The Presence of a Timeless God', *Faith and Philosophy* 24 (2007): 3–27 (https://place.asburyseminary.edu/faithandphilosophy/vol24/iss1/1/), and then Brian Leftow's defence of a presentist reading in 'Anselmian Presentism', *Faith and Philosophy* 26 (2009): 297–319 (https://place.asburyseminary.edu/faithandphilosophy/vol26/iss3/4/). William E. Mann, 'Anselm on Divine Justice and Mercy', *Religious Studies* 55 (2019): 469–85, offers a sympathetic reconstruction of Anselm's solution to the apparent conflict between divine justice and divine mercy in the *Proslogion*.

Chapter 3: Looking for God

Any standard textbook in the philosophy of religion will offer an account of what I have called the consensus reading of the ontological argument, but the treatment in Michael C. Murray and Michael Rea, *An Introduction to the Philosophy of Religion* (Cambridge: Cambridge University Press, 2008) is especially clear in its presentation both of the argument and of the objections that are most commonly brought against it. The reading of the argument I defend in this chapter is presented more fully in Visser and Williams, *Anselm*, pp. 73–109. Peter van Inwagen offers a powerful and clear exposition of the modal ontological argument and its difficulties in *Metaphysics*, 4th edn (London: Routledge, 2015), pp. 135–58.

Chapter 4: How things got started

See Visser and Williams, *Anselm*, pp. 41–56, for a more extensive discussion of Anselm's account of truth and pp. 123–43 for a discussion of creation and the Word. Gareth Matthews offers a more conventional interpretation of Anselm's relationship to Augustine and the theory of divine ideas in 'Anselm, Augustine, and Platonism' in Davies and Leftow, *The Cambridge Companion to Anselm*. By contrast, Jonathan Stewart McIntosh, 'Speaking of Possibilities: The Theistic Actualism of Anselm's Divine *Locutio*', *Modern Theology* 33 (2017): 213–34, argues that Anselm's metaphor of utterance (*locutio*) distinguishes his theory sharply from the Augustinian account of divine ideas.

Chapter 5: How things went wrong

Anselm's account of freedom has received a great deal of scholarly attention. The most influential alternative to the view offered here (defended in Visser and Williams, *Anselm*, pp. 171–91) has been that of Katherin A. Rogers, especially in *Anselm on Freedom* (Oxford: Oxford University Press, 2008) and *Freedom and Self-Creation: A Libertarian Account* (Oxford: Oxford University

Press, 2017). Two recent articles take up the conceptual difficulties of Anselm's account of the fall of the devil: William Wood, 'Anselm of Canterbury on the Fall of the Devil: The Hard Problem, the Harder Problem, and a New Formal Model of the First Sin', *Religious Studies* 52 (2016): 223–45; Michael Barnwell, 'The "Harder Problem" of the Devil's Fall Is Still a Problem: A Reply to Wood', *Religious Studies* 53 (2017): 521–43.

Chapter 6: The great restoration project

Anselm's account of the atonement is as heavily debated in theology as his ontological argument is in philosophy, and the literature on it is vast. A good place to start is Oliver D. Crisp, *Approaching the Atonement: The Reconciling Work of Christ* (Downers Grove, IL: IVP, 2020). Crisp devotes his fourth chapter to Anselm; his exposition is critical but sympathetic, giving a fair hearing to recent theological criticism of Anselm. Fleming Rutledge, *The Crucifixion: Understanding the Death of Jesus Christ* (Grand Rapids, MI: Eerdmans, 2017), is more of a defender of Anselm than Crisp is, making creative and constructive use of Anselm throughout her work; of particular interest is her chapter 'Anselm Reconsidered for Our Time' (pp. 146–66).

Chapter 7: Living in the meantime

The theoretical foundations of Anselm's ethical theory are well-explored in Jeffrey Brower, 'Anselm on Ethics', in Davies and Leftow, *The Cambridge Companion to Anselm*, pp. 222–56. Sandra Visser and I attempt to connect the theoretical foundations with Anselm's practical advice in *Anselm*, pp. 193–211. Benedicta Ward's introduction to *The Prayers and Meditations of Saint Anselm with the Proslogion* explores in depth the background and spirituality of Anselm's devotional writing.

Index

For the benefit of digital users, indexed terms that span two pages (e.g., 52–53) may, on occasion, appear on only one of those pages.

Anselm